Educating Young Children through Natural Water

D1597358

Coastlines, rivers and natural water have a huge amount to offer young children, providing a unique environment for their learning and development. The environment, and its almost daunting size, touches something deep within the children and – surprisingly – the large space brings them closer together. This book provides a comprehensive guide to Water School provision by exploring its special pedagogy, the organisation and management of Water School sessions, and discussing the learning environment and its implications for children's well-being and development. It clearly explains the key principles of this contemporary approach, recently created by the author, and determines a framework for setting up and leading a Water School programme.

The book shows how the aims and outcomes of early years education, including the Early Years Foundation Stage, can all be achieved within the Water School environment and is supported by examples and case studies throughout. Full of practical suggestions and activities, it includes:

- ideas for outside learning that cover topics such as wildlife, sensory activities, crafts, social development, physical play and construction in different seasons;
- unique teaching tools to observe and develop the children;
- ideas for working with children of different ages and learning styles;
- detailed guidance on health and safety, including risk assessments.

By offering a sound historical background, a solid pedagogical framework and a step-by-step guide to Water School practice, this handy text will help students and practitioners to fully understand this new and increasingly popular approach to early years education and how it can benefit the children they care for.

Judit Horvath is a day nursery manager with Qualified Teacher Status and Early Years Professional Status, currently working on her PhD. She has written widely for magazines such as *Nursery World*, *Teach Nursery*, *Practical Preschool* and *Early Years Educator*, whilst actively practising and developing her Water School approach.

Educating Young Children through Natural Water

How to use coastlines, rivers and lakes to promote learning and development

Judit Horvath

Routledge
Taylor & Francis Group

LONDON AND NEW YORK

First published 2016
by Routledge
2 Park Square, Milton Park, Abingdon, Oxon OX14 4RN

and by Routledge
711 Third Avenue, New York, NY 10017

Routledge is an imprint of the Taylor & Francis Group, an informa business

British Library Cataloguing in Publication Data
A catalogue record for this book is available from the British Library

Library of Congress Cataloging in Publication Data
Horvath, Judit, 1978-
Educating young children through natural water : how to use coastlines, rivers
and lakes to promote learning and development / Judit Horvath.
pages cm
1. Environmental sciences—Study and teaching (Elementary) 2. Bodies of
water—Study and teaching (Elementary) 3. Shorelines—Study and teaching
(Elementary) 4. Sustainable development—Study and teaching (Elementary)
5. Environment and education. 6. Children and the environment. I. Title.
GE70.H67 2016
372.35'7—dc23
2015016814

ISBN: 978-0-415-72890-4 (hbk)
ISBN: 978-0-415-72891-1 (pbk)
ISBN: 978-1-315-67186-4 (ebk)

Typeset in Sabon
by Swales & Willis Ltd, Exeter, Devon, UK

Printed and bound in the United States of America by Publishers Graphics,
LLC on sustainably sourced paper.

43888951

Contents

Chapter 1

The origin and validity of Water School

Water is at the root of all life; without it we cannot survive and as such it connects to us in a root way. Outdoor play should allow children to be surrounded by water based experiences from jumping in a puddle to hearing it trickle over stones.

(Warden, 2007, p. 41)

Introduction

This chapter will explore the innate relationship between humans and water, and note the old traditions that describe water as a necessity in people's lives. It will describe the current social views that inform public opinion about natural water. It will consider why children love water and what makes it an excellent educational resource, while determining what the Water School approach is, with some principles similar to and some different from other outdoor approaches. It will discuss the properties of water in its natural form that provide opportunities to teach young children about their world. The chapter will consider both historical perspectives and contemporary ideas that affect the development of Water School.

What does water mean to humans?

Water has extreme healing potential for the human mind, body, and spirit. Water benefits people physically, biologically, and mentally as it has a therapeutic and refreshing nature. For many years throughout human history, water has been credited with helping to cure illnesses, revitalise the body, and calm and relax the soul and mind. Thales of Miletus, the Greek philosopher, wrote that water is the material source of all living things. The human body is about 75 per cent water, and water covers almost 70 per cent of the world's surface, therefore it is logical to describe water as the elixir of nature. Humans have observed and investigated the healing potential of water with its spiritual, physical, and biological qualities, and the powers of water – concrete and mystical – were appreciated and celebrated by humans for centuries (adapted from Kevin Ebner, 2005).

By analysing the relationship between people and water, three main topics have been shown to have significant roles in the effectiveness of Water School:

1   The physical relationship between humans and water;
2   The innate relationship between humans and water with its psychological impli-
    cations – water as a symbol;
3   Water as an educational resource.

The physical and psychological understanding of water

On the physical level, water benefits the body's systems in many ways. It is taken
in via the mouth, then into the stomach and intestinal tract, and received into the
bloodstream, increasing its volume instantly. Finally, the water is eliminated through
the lungs, skin, kidneys, and intestines. Water, when leaving the body, removes waste
through urinary excretions and the activity of the skin. It also assists in the elimina-
tion of the mucus membrane in the intestinal tract, which is an important organ of
secretion. It relieves, eliminates, stimulates, cleans, and refreshes. It also removes the
foulest materials from the blood, rendering it a blood cleanser for the building up of
tissues, which assists in the waste and repair processes of the body. Bathing increases
the circulation in the body. Water is one of the most powerful means of affecting the
human system in health and disease, having been used frequently for remedial purposes. Hippocrates – the founder of modern medicine – was the first to write widely
about the healing of disease with water. 'Give me the power to create a fever, and I
shall cure any disease,' he boasted, more than 2,000 years ago, referring to balneo-
therapy (bathing in thermal springs), pressure or compressing hydrotherapy (pres-
suring the body with water-flow), thalassotherapy (ocean bath), wet blanket wrap,
and soft sponge bath. The early Egyptians also practised healing in water extensively.
Bathing held a prominent place in the law that was written – under divine instruction – by Moses, for the government of the Hebrew nation. The ancient Persians
and Greeks erected stately and magnificent public buildings devoted to water. The
Romans surpassed all other nations in the cost and magnificence of their wet facilities, some of their greatest works of architecture being their public baths (adapted
from King's Psychology Network, n.d.). Two noted Latin physicians, Celus and
Galen, praised and glorified water as being invaluable (Kloss, 1939). In 1600, public
vapour baths were plentiful in Paris. Furthermore, many early hospitals would give
steam and water baths. According to historical records (Looman and Pillen, 1989),
the Germans were very fond of bathing, and during the Middle Ages it was a religious
duty to bathe because of the national faith in the cleaning power of water (Kloss,
1939, p. 104).
    Water is one of the most effective mediums for human thought processing, due to
its mental and emotional effects on people; it has a unique ability to lift the spirit. The
fluidity of water is the best natural representation of emotions; its turbulent sea waves
and ever-flowing rivers have inspired many artists throughout history. The surface of
the water evolves into waves that can be gentle and slow, or unpredictable and life-
threatening. Deeper, beneath the surface of the water, one can find quiet calmness
and, as opposed to its often wild surface, the relaxed environment beneath the water
hosts many interesting and beautiful life forms. Water represents the human subconscious. In comparison to the water, the human mind encompasses a world in its

deepest subconscious but, like the beings in the water, we can only glimpse it briefly. The subconscious is filled with the unknown. The imagery of the subconscious is likened to the imagery of artists' ways of thinking about water, with symbols holding deeper meanings that affect us on an emotional level. The watery womb is nurturing and life-sustaining. Going 'back into the womb' is a phrase that implies calmness, comfort, security, and a level of familiarity. Young children have a closer relationship with their psyche and their internal thought processing, resulting in their self-driven thought-provocation that is effortless and natural. At the start of human life, the womb reflects the creative qualities of water. The 'tiny watery individual' is able to develop on many levels simultaneously, just as people develop a creative project over time. Jung used the concept of water as inspiration for his 'Feelings' category of human psychology.

> Water is the commonest symbol for the unconscious. The lake in the valley is the unconscious, which lies, as it were, underneath consciousness, so that it is often referred to as the 'subconscious,' usually with the pejorative connotation of an inferior consciousness. Water is the 'valley spirit,' the water dragon of Tao, whose nature resembles water – a yang in the yin, therefore, water means spirit that has become unconscious.
>
> (Jung, 1991)

In order to create inner peace one should be at peace with the unconscious, which is one of the main reasons for humans having a close relationship with water throughout history.

Based on water's properties, nurturing children close to water – in all its forms – will strengthen their inner processing skills, widen their understanding of their own psyche, while providing experiences of undefined media for human discovery, personal expression, and success. The river embodies the flow of life; as the 'teleology' of Jungian therapy says, it strengthens the goal-directedness of the psyche (Jung, 1991). It also embodies the clear, powerful, one-way direction of the flow of our lives. Water as rain symbolises a new beginning, cleansing, and belonging – a crucial aspect of our experience of water. In many cultures with limited rainfall there is a mystical, magic power attached to rainfall. Large bodies of water – oceans, lakes, and pools – can symbolise the unconscious that helps children, and all humans, to accept their own unknown; this represents the concept that, as with bodies of water, we often see the surface, but cannot easily see into the depths. Accepting their own unknown is a necessary act in order to achieve inner peace, as the unconscious mind is much larger than the conscious part. Water lacks structure, limit, and exact definition; it can be whatever a child wants it to be. There is no right or wrong way to play with it or in it, and in its natural state it is full of extremes and opposites, familiar and unfamiliar features that provide limitless opportunities for education.

In some parts of the world water is the cheapest, most abundant, and easily accessible resource we have. Today, however, the closest thing many humans have to a spiritual aquatic experience is a quick shower at some point in their busy day.

Water as a symbol

Throughout history, water has always been used to symbolise different things in different parts of the world. Water is a universal symbol of going forward, change, purity, cleansing, life, death, clarity, and the unknown, often marking something dramatic, both positive and negative. Interestingly, it can be used to symbolise completely opposing theories at the same time; for example, water can represent good health, but also can represent things being rotten and dated. In literature, water appears in various forms: the river is a sign of grace, fluidity, and lightness, with its calm beauty; a fast-flowing river can often be used to symbolise strength, power, change, and understanding; a slow-flowing river can often be used to symbolise weakness, but also steadiness; the ocean is a symbol of immense power and strength, dominating all other images of water. All life is ocean-born and life still exists in the ocean. Large bodies of water represent mystery, being unpredictable and uncontrollable, hard to navigate, stormy, but also beautifully calm, dictated purely by its own will. Sometimes, the ocean is referred to as being a tear of God, or sorrow; a place where humans leave bad memories and sadness. The ocean is also known to symbolise hope, truth, and in some cases magic. The ocean's salt can also symbolise being well-grounded or stabilised.

For many centuries, different cultures have appreciated that the average human body is 55–78 per cent water. Babies have the most, being born with about 78 per cent. By one year of age, that proportion drops to about 65 per cent. In adult men, about 60 per cent of their bodies are water. Thus water represents existence, circulation, life, cohesion, and birth, by associating the creative waters of the earth with the fluids found in our own bodies. The ancient Greeks often observed the power of transition that water possesses, trying to understand how it transforms from solid, to liquid, to vapour. In their understanding, water is the symbol for metamorphosis and philosophical recycling. The ancient Egyptians celebrated their beloved Nile River as being akin to the birth canal of their existence. In Taoist tradition, water is considered an aspect of wisdom. The concept states that water takes on the form in which it is held, and then gradually moves in the path of least resistance, being the symbolic meaning of higher wisdom. The indigenous people of North America considered water a valuable commodity, a symbol of life, further using the symbol with similar meaning in many creation myths.

Water is a strong element of classic folk tales, which have an important role in knowledge transfer and personality development. Classic folk tales were tools to influence children's perception, attitude, behaviour, and many other factors important to human life as well as society, which can be concluded as follows (Prayon Songsilp, 1999, p. 6):

- Folk tales help people to better understand general conditions of humanity, since they are sources of constructed perceptions, beliefs, paradigms, fear, fun, and formality.
- Folk tales were used to communicate boundaries and guidelines for people's lives in society, to show the difference between right and wrong, and to install discipline from childhood.
- Folk tales, while entertaining, enable children to learn about local lifestyles, national heritage, and culture, leading to social pride, unity, and harmony.

- Folk tales are both art and science, being the origin of various sciences that widened learning in other fields of study; this is a possible way of educating through natural water.

'The Water of Life' is a German fairy tale collected by the Brothers Grimm. In this fairy tale there was a king who was dying. The old man told his sons that the water of life would save him. Each one set out in turn. The two older ones, setting out in hope of being made the heir, were rude to a dwarf on the way and became trapped in ravines; however the youngest son, through many adventures, found the water. His brothers tried to trick him and get him killed, by making the king sick with sea water. In the end, however, all sinister acts came to light, and a good deed gained its reward. In this story the metaphorical issues of growth, change, and healing are explored. The king's sickness represents changes in viewpoints and perspectives, meaning people change with the changing world. Being unable to adapt and not being honest – like the older brothers – will prevent mental growth. Failing to listen to our inner thoughts, as symbolised by the dwarf, will prove to be an obstacle in life. The young prince, who stops and thinks, willing to courageously set out on a journey into an unknown, deeper emotional life, becomes master of his own life and acquires treasures that will ensure emotionally healthy change and healing comes to his life. The water of life, itself, symbolises the essence of life. The prince finds it, but before he can bring it back to his father, his brothers steal his healing power and claim it as their own. This reminds people not to let success go to their heads. The two older brothers represent ego, arrogance, and misused power. They cannot, however, keep this false self-image, because they have no knowledge of helping others, being unable to distinguish between right and wrong.

There is also a Catalan fairy tale entitled 'The Water of Life', collected by D. Francisco de S. Maspons y Labros, and included by Andrew Lang in his collection of fairy and folk tales, *The Pink Fairy Book*. This tale also represents emotional growth, with similar elements: listening to inner thoughts, bravely following life's path, finding happiness in small treasures and beauty, sharing success. The story tells of three brothers and a sister, who worked very hard, became rich, and built a palace, much admired; but when told by an old woman it needed a church, they built one. An old man told them it needed a pitcher of the water of life, a branch where the smell of the flowers gives eternal beauty, and a talking bird, representing material things in life that are worthless without inner beauty. The oldest brother decided to search for these things; his progress was indicated on a knife from the old man: as long as it was bright, he was well, but when it was bloody, evil had happened to him. He met a giant who told him he had to walk past stones that would mock him; if he did not turn around, he could achieve what he was after, but if he did, he would also turn to stone. He went to the mountain, but the stones jeered at him so loudly that he turned to throw a rock at them, and was himself turned to stone. Warned by the knife that something had happened, his two brothers followed him, and suffered the same fate. Their sister followed, but did not turn. At the top of the mountain she found a pool, and the bird perched on a branch of the tree. She took the bird and the branch, but was tired; as she collected some of the water, she spilled a few drops on the stones, which turned the brothers back to life. She sprinkled more of the water on the remaining stones and restored all the people to life. At home she planted the tree and watered it. It grew, and the bird perched in its boughs. A prince came to see the wonders and married the sister in the church they had built.

In the Korean folk tale, *The Magic Spring*, an old, hard-working couple are often laughed at by their rich, greedy neighbour for not having a child; but they never complain, are always kind, and often find time to admire nature's beauty. One day a bird leads the old man to a clear spring from which he drinks, regaining his youth; he takes his wife there; she also drinks just enough to become young again. Upon the greedy neighbour's questioning they tell him the secret of the water but warn him to only take a sip, but he fails to listen to their advice and never returns. When they try to find him, next to the neighbour's cloak they discover a tiny baby, who they raise with love and kindness as their own. In this comparison of the kind and the greedy, water represents renewed energy and life. As in other folk tales, when attention is paid to the presence of a new thought in the heart, represented by the song, life gains new meaning. When only seeing results without working on finding life's personalised song, life becomes pointless and bitter. The tale also shows, through water, that too much of a good thing, especially when not earned, may result in unwanted turns in life. Although water represents wanted and unwanted change, the meaning of water as potential for transformation, is acceptable in any form, highlighting water as a symbol of hope.

The use of water as a symbol does not have clearly defined guidelines or rules. Authors use it in different ways, representing different thoughts and meanings, to highlight different factors of importance. It is always versatile, and yet it never changes; it gives constant fuel to the fires of imagination. Literature will never be able to do without it, and in all probability, water will always symbolise new and unchanging things in the future.

Water and children

Unstructured free play outdoors brings a host of benefits to children, from becoming smarter, to being more cooperative, and healthier overall. Water is a common but extremely exciting material that is freely available almost everywhere and, being an open-ended resource, lends itself to an almost endless variety of children's activities. Although common in its appearance and sourcing possibilities, water is one of the most brilliant sources of child exploration that host magic, wonder, and exploration for humans of all ages. Water is pleasant, comfortable, and frames simple baby activities as much as the more complex science experiments of school-age children. It gives children the opportunity to exert control from an early age; it is both familiar and mysterious. Children around water can be observant and active, quiet and loud, slow and quick, weak and strong; water allows for all abilities and personalities. Water, especially in its natural environment, has an effect on all the senses: sight, hearing, taste, smell, and touch.

When thoughtfully planned and prepared, water-related activities – especially outdoors with no restrictions – can support a range of developmental areas. Children have a natural, inbuilt motivation to make sense of the world around them. Opportunity-rich environments, with materials that children can easily and freely manipulate, support children's cognitive development and aid the brain in creating and strengthening neural pathways. Based on this foundation, children's brains can form the frameworks through which important life-concepts are learnt. When spending time in surprising and unpredictable environments, children face information that does not make sense in their previously built frameworks, creating cognitive dissonance, so they have to restart the process, adjust their way of thinking and form new concepts; therefore the process accommodates and stimulates learning. Exploration of this kind needs time, space, and people to share sustained thinking with. Water gives opportunity to children to explore a wide range of mathematical concepts (empty–full, heavy–light, big–small, sinking–floating, shallow–deep, etc.) providing a base for practising necessary skills such as sorting, counting, and measuring. During this process children learn language naturally; they learn new words to make sense of their newly developed concepts. When they are encouraged to use this vocabulary by repetition of opportunity, a deep level of learning is achieved naturally. Water play and its related activities also naturally lead children to ask questions when they encounter unknown concepts. If answered in the appropriate manner, that encourages them to be curious; curiosity itself will lead to experimentation and perseverance, stimulating further curiosity and learning, to explore and understand the environment, characteristics, and science of water. This process can accommodate all types of play – solitary, parallel, and a variety of social play: associative and cooperative – but in all its forms, playing around water ensures children have some kind of connection to others.

Water play promotes healthy development through the use of small and large muscles, coordination, and spatial awareness. Water play offers endless enjoyment for children. The phrase 'being in our element' originally refers to basic experiments with natural elements, such as water and its surroundings.

Water as an educational resource: modern nature and outdoor education theories (adapted from James Neill's work (2004))

Theorists and thinkers have long been analysing the elements, process, and importance of outdoor education and learning. Although these thinkers have not exclusively researched water as an educational resource, they have observed nature and natural environments as a whole, their theories building the foundation for education through and with natural water.

The Australian researcher James Neill's *Psycho-Evolutionary Theory of Outdoor Education* (2004) has been working on reviewing traditional and modern nature education theories; he outlines the categories of nature education, summarised in three major groups:

1　environmental theories
2　experimental theories
3　psycho-social theories.

Environmental theories emphasise the effects of nature on people

Outdoor education in general is characterised by direct engagement with natural environments and indirect engagement via adventurous activities within those natural environments. Many outdoor education theories could be called nature theories, based on outdoor education as a basic human experience, emphasising that 'returning to nature' is good. This way of thinking is often referred to as the 'Garden of Eden' theory. Throughout hundreds of years, shifting from urbanised, complex environments to more natural environments has been appreciated as valuable for relaxing, calming, healing, re-connecting, and strengthening people. Research findings in health, medicine, and psychology also appear to be supportive of the proposition that nature has some inherently positive effects on physical and psychological well-being for humans (and other animals). As Neill states (2005), two of the best-known modern researchers in this area are Robert Ulrich – who has researched the effects of natural vistas on his own hospital patients – and Dr Howard S. Frumkin – who has reviewed the leading research literature on the physical health benefits of natural environments. Many of Neill's theories refer to the most popular, scientific-type beliefs, and in his scientific work he analysed the 'nature is good' hypothesis (2005). Among many others, Neill summarised Edward O. Wilson's work, with special attention to his biophilia hypothesis, which described the positive effects of nature that – probably – based on humanity's long evolutionary and biological links is the reason for a human's strong need to be in natural environments. According to Wilson, 'Humanity is exalted not because we are so far above other living creatures, but because knowing them well elevates the very concept of life' (Wilson, 1984: 22).

Wilson's biophilia hypothesis has been debated and critiqued. One of the issues appears to be that Wilson based his ideas on his study of insects and that the idea is too simplistic to fully account for humanity's relationship with natural environments, since humans have also shown a capacity to adapt to artificial environments.

Neill has also reviewed the work of Peter Martin (currently head of the outdoor education programme at La Trobe University, Australia, the largest outdoor education department in the world) who has a modern and well-developed, caring-based relationship model for understanding outdoor education. Martin viewed the nature–human relationship from the process point of view, analysing what actually happens to humans in the natural environment. He stated that the process is an active conversation between person and environment that evolves over time. In this sense, many visits over a period of time to a natural place are recommended over one-off visits to novel natural places. For example, climbing at a particular place during different seasons and weather conditions over many years creates a significant, relational understanding of that natural place by the person. Peter Martin has recently completed his PhD on this topic (Neill, 2005). Wilderness settings and related activities are vehicles through which one can find something out about oneself (Scherl, 1988).

Being outside normal, familiar contexts frees up previous habitual constraints, heightens arousal and focus, and encourages experimentation with 'new psychological strategies or a fresh sense of identity' (Kimball and Bacon, 1993: 26). Another environmental mechanism is the novelty and unpredictability of remote, wilderness environments. Intervention programmes which take place in unfamiliar environments have greater effects (Hattie, 1992).

Psychological and phenomenological processes of the nature experience

Dewey stated that the task for education is the guided direction of students' natural impulses. A balance needs to be struck between the freedom of individuals and the educative structure of the learning environment. Dewey has expressed this approach in many of his writings: 'To find out what one is fitted to do and to secure an opportunity to do it is the key to happiness' (Dewey, 2012: 208).

In their work about experiential learning, Gibbons and Hopkins (1980), and later Horton and Hutchinson (1997), also emphasised the point made powerfully in John Dewey's theory of experience (2012): that life and learning is 100 per cent experiential. Gibbons and Hopkins inspired followers to define experiential learning, given that '. . . all learning is experiential' (Joplin 1985: 155). One is experientially engaged in every moment, whatever type of experience it is. Experientiality isn't switched off and on like a light switch. Gibbons and Hopkins' desire was to point out the different kinds of engagements a person may have with educational experiences; they demonstrated a preference for activities in which the study is heavily engaged in the planning and process. These are seen as more active, whereas they imply that there are significant limitations and lack of experientiality for educational activities where the participant 'receives' rather than interacts. However, some other research – for example, post-modern literary analysis – reveals that reading of texts or watching images, is far from passive (Guillory, 1995: 44).

Kolb's four-stage experiential learning style theory (1984) is represented by a cycle in which the learner 'touches all the bases': the Concrete Experience, which is a new experience of a situation or a reinterpretation of existing experience; the Reflective Observation of the new experience is of particular importance with inconsistencies between experience and understanding; the Abstract Conceptualisation, when a reflection gives rise to a new idea, or a modification of an existing abstract concept, and the Active Experimentation when the learner applies them to the world around them.

Most outdoor education and adventure-based programmes share a theoretical emphasis on experiential learning principles, although there is no clear agreement on which of the several different types of experiential learning cycles is most relevant to outdoor education. The three-stage model, 'do–review–plan', seems to best satisfy the law of parsimony (the simplest of two or more theories is preferable).

Social support and group development in the natural environment

Building psychological resilience is an underlying intention of 'development-by-stress' or 'stress inoculation' training philosophies, such as is in outdoor education programmes. Kurt Hahn (1957) referred to the difficult, challenging nature of Outward Bound courses, for example, as a double-edged sword that cut and healed the participant, making them even stronger. To become resilient, we need to engage in experiences that cut us mentally and physically, but leave us stronger for it.

James Neill's *Psycho-Evolutionary Theory of Outdoor Education* (2004) proposes that our behaviours, attitudes, cognitions, and emotions, are shaped by what proved adaptive during human evolution, i.e. the forces of natural selection have significantly shaped our psychological state. Outdoor education has emerged out of two forces:

our evolutionary history, and the rapid cultural shift away from the natural living forces of nature. These forces have created a perfect storm, and outdoor education has emerged in post-industrial Western societies as a semi-ritualistic, compensatory effort for humans to re-engage with their indigenous heritage and inner indigenous nature. Outdoor education, in a way, bridges the two worlds by taking people from Western world lifestyles into a world with less technology and requiring more basic, physical, and psychological self-reliance and direct engagement in hands-on survival-type tasks with others.

In recent centuries, humans have rapidly evolved artificial living environments. The rapid departure from relatively natural living environments has left strong vestigial physiological and psychological remnants of connections to nature, which still predominantly drive people. However, since the biological needs of most people are reasonably well catered for in post-industrial societies, people in these societies have leisure time, a significant portion of which they use to engage in activities that bring them several steps back toward natural environments and activities that were akin to those of their ancestors.

Hattie, Marsh, Neill, and Richards (1997) proposed four theoretical elements, which they suggested be further investigated: the immediately engaging nature of adventurous outdoor experiences that emphasise a 'here and now' focus for participants and gets them actively involved; the difficult, but achievable, goals that are set with substantial support to help participants achieve these difficult goals; a large amount of high-quality feedback to the learner through their own actions, through the behaviour of others, from the instructor, from the tasks, and from the environment; and the reassessment of an individual's coping skills, which requires adaptation and learning of new coping skills. Neill, Hattie and other researchers also noted that there is surprisingly little theoretical literature in outdoor education emphasising the relationship that occurs between individuals and elements of the natural environment during outdoor education experiences.

What is Water School?

Water School is a brand new concept and is a natural adjunct to Forest School. As a pedagogy and as a physical entity, Forest School is an outdoor education approach that utilises natural woodlands and in which children regularly visit forests, learning personal and technical skills. These skills are delivered by trained leaders, following a set educational programme, and by placing the learner at the heart of the learning experience both Water and Forest schools promote holistic, individualised learning and development. The pedagogical approach, common to Water and Forest schools, allows participants to take responsibility for their own learning and development. The impacts on behaviour, motivation, and learning are positive for all, but particularly for those who find a traditional classroom environment challenging. The student-led learning ethos in Water School is the same as it is in Forest School, but the surroundings are different. Water Schools value and encourage independence, which in turn enhances self-confidence and self-esteem. Participants are encouraged to assess risks inherent in the environment and in activities. While safety and well-being are, of course, paramount, it is essential to value learning opportunities presented by apparently risky activities. For example, walking across potentially slippery surfaces develops a sense of balance while discovering appropriate ways of traversing the terrain. Water School learners become more knowledgeable, more empathetic, and develop greater respect and appreciation of the coastal environment. Participating in Water Schools encourages a profound understanding of our role as guardians of this precious environment.

It is usually a long-term programme delivered by trained Water School leaders within a natural beach environment; there are regular (usually weekly) visits to the same beach. Each Water School programme is tailored to meet the needs of individuals within that group and is continuously developed as the children grow in confidence, skills, and understanding.

Sessions are not timetable- or workbook-led; instead they are led by the children themselves using their interests and imagination. However, sessions are structured through qualified leaders. This sort of outdoor-based learning can be complementary and not separate from learning in a traditional classroom environment.

What does natural water mean to people?

During the development of my Water School provision, a small-scale qualitative research study was carried out using questionnaires. In this process, the parents in my nursery setting were asked to provide a short answer to four questions:

> *What does natural water mean to you?*
>
> *What forms of natural water do you visit and why?*
>
> *What does local natural water mean to you personally?*
>
> *Do you find natural wet areas important and why?*

These questionnaires may not have been the most robust method to collect qualitative data, as the requirement to respond to the provocative questions could have resulted in people not acting naturally. However, collecting the information from a wider – but still local and relevant – sample of population was reached by personal interviews. The information was limited to the formation of my particular Water School provision, but it is very useful, providing background directly from the provision users. The questionnaire explored general opinions. This questionnaire can be used in the first instance, followed by informative parents' meetings, open programmes, and gatherings, generating interaction between different techniques.

The answers were analysed and scanned for key features; findings were then grouped based on similarities in the answers to provide data about what natural water means to people.

> *Emotional value:* childhood, memory, history, family, friends, holiday, relaxing, community, national treasure.
>
> *Sensory and physical value*: freedom, natural beauty, sunshine, fresh air, water, joy.
>
> *Personal interest:* dog-walking, fishing, being in nature, preserving nature's treasures, hobby (collection, observation, photography, bird watching).

Life necessities and life quality improvers: commuting to work, job, being out-doors/health, activities/exercises/sport (running, walking, swimming).

The majority of people who visit natural water today were introduced to rivers, streams, and the sea as a young child. In my nursery, the children's experience of natural water involves three kinds of contact: direct, indirect, and artificial play experience. Within our Water School provision, children have opportunities to interact directly with uncontrolled, spontaneous, unplanned natural features and processes that are untouched by human involvement and occur in the water's natural environment (plants, animals, and habitats). Children also encounter indirect experiences of natural water that occur in created and highly controlled environments that depend on ongoing human management and intervention. Indirect experiences of nature are planned, resourced, structured, and organised with occasional elements of other living – not wild – beings (pets). These indirect experiences of nature occur through the mud kitchen, the wormery, water play, gardening, looking after pets, and controlled habitats. The artificial play experience of nature does not involve contact with actual living organisms or environments but rather with the image, representation, or metaphorical expression of nature in factual and story books, magazines, drawings, photos, and other art, music/sound, CDs, and computer games.

Chapter 2

The environments and ecosystems of Water School

Introduction

This chapter will outline the diversity of natural water: including the shallow, deep, and flowing forms that can be considered as environments for Water School: the river, the chalk stream, the lake, the wetland, the sea, and the garden pond, highlighting the geological and biological characteristics of these environments that enable practitioners to educate children. It examines the ecological systems of these locations, which can provide educational opportunities for the Water School programme. It will give a basic understanding of these ecological systems to emphasise how they can inform teaching practice.

The idea of Water School stems from the widely used and celebrated outdoor education approach, Forest School. However, there are significant differences between the two approaches, which all stem from the environment:

1 more rapid change of habitat, immediate changes within hours;
2 an increased level of freedom: holistic; freedom of touch, body, soul, emotions, and freedom of voice and expression; freedom of movement – the use of Laban theory in Water School;
3 more direct contact with a wider variety of wildlife 'on show', always live, always moving.

Even regular users, visitors, and lovers of nature and natural water are often unaware how fragile the water habitats really can be. Several species of birds, fish, amphibians, insects, and mammals use natural water as their home, which is why it is important to keep these habitats healthy and to understand how to sustain them for hundreds of years to come. It is also necessary to view natural water in its wider local environments – including the surrounding terrain – as they maintain the transition from land to the body of water. All plants existing near natural water – rivers, creeks, streams, and any other water sources – need to help sustain the river and the life that depends on it. They create a strong root system in the shoreline, being instrumental in preventing erosion. The tall grass and trees provide a habitat where many species can find shade from an unseasonably hot day and are useful in maintaining a cooler water temperature. These habitats offer many diverse places to live, feed, and breed for many species of animals. They are home to migratory birds and migratory fish, which use the banks of rivers for hiding and feeding along their journey. Islands along rivers also provide a welcoming home for wildlife. If children understand the life behind what they see, they may cause less major disruption to the habitat in their future years, eliminating man-made buildings that block the proper flow of the water, which prevents several species of fish from reaching their desired spawning grounds. The combination of riparian forests, bay grasses, wetlands, islands, and numerous other habitats have helped to provide healthy rivers across the world.

Natural water has many different forms in our environment: rivers, streams, brooks, springs, ponds, lakes, seas, and oceans. Although the names and some of the characteristics are varied, all the flora and fauna have to cope with the same thing: water that flows, moves, cools, warms, freezes, and changes continuously. Plants and animals have to be able to cling on, hide away or swim against the current. Picturesque streams, powerful rivers, huge waterfalls, and vast oceans all represent an impressive diversity of our natural watercourses, with a variety of flow patterns, channels, and water beds, as well as a range of different bank habitats.

Water is a medium of extreme properties that strongly influence and shape the nature of the living beings that thrive in it, and life in the water requires special characteristics: the ability to change and adapt rapidly.

The river (adapted from Wildlife Trusts – Habitat Explorer)

Rivers are essential to people's daily lives, providing water for drinking, for industry, and also highly valued landscapes, recreational areas, the experience of nature, and an alternative place for those wanting to reconnect with natural water. River networks across the world provide various habitats for a colourful water and wetland wildlife. Over many centuries, rivers have been manipulated by straightening, widening, deepening, and damming, mainly to improve the drainage of land for housing, industry, and farmland, and to reduce the risk of local flooding. As a result of this human activity, river and bank-side habitats have become affected and the large variety of natural wildlife they support has changed or disappeared. Stream systems play an important role in the biological cycle, transporting water off the landscape to the estuaries and oceans. The role of rivers and creeks is greater than simple drainage, however, providing unique habitat for many species of aquatic flora and fauna. Rivers and streams also act as links between different habitats. The wide network of flowing water can create the perfect site for Water School provision.

Rivers can be generally divided into two groups, based on their location. Upland areas of running water are typically steep, with a bed of rock and pebbles. These rivers can present an extremely powerful flow, influenced by natural forces such as heavy rain and melting snow. The water of these rivers is crystal-clear, due to the low nutrient content that provides for sparse vegetation such as mosses. Insects and birds can be found around these waters, with their typical fish population being salmon and trout.

The rivers and streams of lowland areas have many more nutrients in their flowing water. The river beds are made up of sand and are home to a wide range of water plants. Among them the most popular are pickerelweed, water hyacinth, and arrowhead (duck potato). Shallow streams can support water chestnut, a plant that has leaves above and below the surface. Some plants have adapted to live predominantly beneath the water's surface (submerged), some float on the surface (floating), others emerge from the water with stiff stems holding the plant's leaves above the water (emergent). There are grasses, sedges, (prairie cord grass, sedge), and wild flowers (cattails, arrowheads, duckweed, vervain, marigold, skunk cabbage).

Chub, dace, roach, perch, eel, carp, and pike all live in these waters, together with crabs, crayfish, and freshwater mussels. These rich supplies attract and feed many predators, for example otter, mink, weasel, and heron. Other animals such as frogs, birds, and snails, together with small and larger mammals (water vole, rat, shrew, badger, bat, deer, fox, squirrel, hedgehog, mouse, polecat) are also very interesting for children to study.

Lower level, downstream waters, have even more nutrients, and rivers often become sluggish, however the diversity of living beings increases with aquatic plants such as water crowfoot and water-milfoil providing cover for fish, and the early adult stages of insects such as damselflies and dragonflies. Seasonally, in times of floods, wet meadows along the banks of these rivers provide vital habitat for breeding animals, as well as a habitat for wild flowers.

The education of children using rivers plays a key role in their development, but even more significantly it is now more important for the rivers than ever before. There are now fewer and fewer rivers around the world where humans have not had a negative impact, and even those few continue to be threatened by many human factors. Canalisation and plant removal – so called cleaning – has led to bank erosion, and pollution. Damming and straightening has caused the devastation of species through the loss of their extremely important hiding, breeding, and feeding places. Dam and reservoir construction has changed water flows, and the introduction of foreign species of plants and animals has had irreversible effects on the native wildlife.

The biological zones of rivers

The waterway networks and their towpaths create valuable green corridors, connecting various wildlife sites and habitats. They allow animals to move freely, and often take the heart of the countryside into urban areas, which makes it possible for various educational settings to set up a Water School provision near natural water.

Although many fresh flowing waters were or are shaped and changed for industrial and agricultural purposes, even small waterway channels can be valuable aquatic wildlife habitats. Different parts of the brooks and rivers are colonised by different plants and animals. Different types of flows – slow and fast – as well as managed water levels, can provide unique habitats that can become vital resources for wildlife.

The *brook/river banks*, where land and water meet, are particularly valuable for biodiversity. The structure and vegetation cover provide habitats for a wide variety of wildlife, including dragonflies, water birds, squirrels, foxes, and hedgehogs. Narrow, flower-rich towpath verges expand in some places and support a rich variety of flora and fauna. They can be important oases for local wildlife in urban areas, and shelter for a variety of insects.

The *hedgerows* along the water's edge were often planted by the original canal companies, and are therefore some of the oldest established habitats, creating shelter and food for many animals. They can also act as corridors between isolated habitats providing shelter for the animals as they move between sites.

The cutting and the *embankment* are essential parts of a river environment's structure and the waterway network. The habitats on slopes include rock exposures, grassland, trees, and scrub. Grassy embankment areas are particularly suitable for wild flowers, including cowslips and orchids, and there is a rich insect fauna associated with this kind of grassland vegetation.

Chalk streams (adapted from Wildlife Trusts – Habitat Explorer)

A stream, in general, is a body of moving water confined by a bottom (or bed) and earthen sides (or banks). There are many categories of streams including creeks, brooks, tributaries, and bayous, varying in size, depth, water-flow, environment, and location. Streams are always changing as the water flows downhill. They are responsible for a great deal of erosion and can create large canyons over time, moving soil and pebbles along with the water.

With their unique characteristics (crystal-clear waters, white-flowering river water crowfoot, and lush bankside vegetation) chalk streams are globally rare habitats, the most iconic of which are to be found in the United Kingdom. They are under threat with the increasing population and growing demand for water. In England chalk streams are located in south and east England – in Dorset, Hampshire, Wiltshire, Kent, Norfolk, south Cambridgeshire, and Hertfordshire, for example. There are also some important chalk streams on the wolds in Lincolnshire and Yorkshire.

There are only around 200 chalk streams in the world, and 85 per cent of these are found in England. The chalk streams have characteristic features that accommodate special wildlife habitats and species. They are fed from groundwater, so the supplying water is very clear and of high quality, creating an abundance of insects, which in turn provide food for fish species. Well vegetated banks and channels create shelter for different species away from predators. Chalk streams are important habitats for brown trout, salmon, otter, water vole, kingfisher, water shrew, and white-clawed crayfish. Chalk streams are also home to special plant communities, with plants such as watercress along the margins. The vegetation, the crystal-clear water and the richness of animal species, make chalk streams visually pleasing and perfect educational resources. Streams, as well as other rivers, suffer from damaging human activities such as milling, abstraction of drinking water, and pollution due to agriculture. These have detrimental effects on the quality and clarity of streams, even resulting in streams virtually disappearing.

The sections of streams

Streams can be very interesting educationally, given the great variety of landscape and habitat their different parts provide and support. The *source*, from where the stream originates, can often be a spring or the top of a mountain. Streams join in *confluences*, creating a different landscape and habitat when two or more streams meet. *Pools* in streams are larger, deeper, and slower parts where the body of water moves differently. All streams run into a large body of water, such as the sea or a lake. These areas are called *estuaries*, and they often form unique ecosystems where water from the stream and the lake or ocean – with their different types of water – mix together.

The lake and pond (adapted from Wildlife Trusts – Habitat Explorer)

Ponds and lakes can come in all shapes and sizes, and occur in a variety of habitats. In a simplified way, ponds and lakes can be defined as smaller or larger bodies of inland water. Ponds are defined as small, permanent, or seasonal water bodies that are up to two hectares in size (UK Biodiversity Action Plan, 1994). To be considered a pond, the body of water must be shallow enough for the vegetation living at the bottom to be able to reach the surface – biologically called the photic zone – or to receive sufficient sunlight to thrive.

Some ponds and lakes are considered as priority habitats, being of high conservation or ecological importance, home to species that are particularly endangered, have exceptional habitat, or have other attributes such as being rare, old, or part of a special landscape.

Ponds are widespread throughout the world and support an immense number of plants and animals; many priority species are associated with them. They are a particularly good habitat for invertebrates and, as pond dipping proves, for many other species as well. The vegetation in ponds and lakes varies according to location, size, and depth. Plants such as yellow water-lily are typical of deeper water, while rush, greater pond sedge, and yellow iris are more characteristic of marginal, shallower areas. Ponds provide important homes for amphibians, for example the protected great crested newt and common toad. They are also home to water voles, snakes, and bats. Waterbirds such as swans, moorhens, and ducks rely on ponds for feeding and nesting, while waders feed on the margins. Ponds provide stepping stones between isolated patches of habitat, linking up the countryside and allowing wildlife to move about freely. They account for an estimated 3 per cent of the world's surface. Recent research shows that a large number of wildlife ponds are in a poor state and many ponds were lost in the last century. The effects of this loss of wildlife ponds are detrimental as freshwater ponds provide many species with suitable breeding and feeding habitats. There are still many existing man-made threats to ponds and lakes all over the world: the introduction of alien species, urban development and land use, agricultural drainage, fragmentation, sewage, and even feeding of ducks.

The biological zones of ponds and lakes

The aquatic environment is shaped by complex interactions between a variety of physical, chemical, and biological factors, such as climate, land topography, bedrock geology, or soil type. These factors support a community of biological organisms unique to a water environment.

The ecosystem of a lake is divided into three distinct sections: the littoral zone, which is the sloped area closest to the edge of the water; the open-water zone (also called the photic or limnetic zone), where sunlight is abundant; and the deep-water zone (also called the aphotic or profundal zone), where little or no sunlight can reach.

The *lake shore* (or *littoral zone*) is the shallow area along the shoreline of a lake or pond, which supports diverse communities of rooted plants and serves as food, habitat, and protective shelter for fish, insects, amphibians, and other aquatic animals. These diverse plant communities also provide cover and nesting materials for a variety of wild birds and mammals. Management of littoral zones is often necessary in systems altered by humans to manage problems such as shoreline erosion, algal blooms, overgrowth of invasive plants, and removal of protective vegetation needed for fish habitat and cover.

Other plants and fish (such as bass and trout) live in the *open-water zone*. The *deep-water zone* does not support the growth of plants, therefore fewer living beings are able to adapt to and cope with living there. In this zone, most organisms are scavengers, such as crabs and catfish, which feed on dead organisms that sink gradually to the bottom of the water. Fungi and bacteria aid the decomposition of those dead organisms.

The wetlands (adapted from Wildlife Trusts – Habitat Explorer)

Wetland refers to land that holds a large amount of water for significant periods of time, and therefore produces specific habitats and creates unique ecosystems that are able to adapt to the extreme wet conditions. Wetlands are usually located between bodies of water and dry land, in varying environments. They can be found in large flat areas as well as small or sloped areas. Wetlands are important for their biological diversity, and are very fragile, being highly sensitive to the water quality.

A *marsh* is a type of shallow wetland usually found around lakes, ponds, streams, or the ocean (therefore either freshwater or saltwater); they are covered with grasses that provide habitat for frogs, turtles, fish, and many varieties of birds.

A *swamp* is a wetland with trees beside slow-moving rivers, frequently or permanently covered with water. Swamps can be freshwater, saltwater, or a mixture of both. With extremely slow-moving water and low oxygen content, the creatures living in it need to be able to adapt and tolerate extreme conditions.

An *estuary* is a wetland where saltwater from the sea mixes with freshwater from a stream or river. Its plants and animals can adapt to drastic changes influenced by the content and movement of the water. Due to the different levels of salt content in the waters of the different areas of an estuary, many different habitats can live closely together, creating an extremely rich biodiversity.

The sea and beaches (adapted from Wildlife Trusts – Habitat Explorer)

The sea itself is obviously not a primary focus for working with children; education is rather concentrated on the beaches. The coast is a more general term referring to the junction of land and water, but a beach is made of specific materials such as sand, cobbles, or shells.

A beach is a narrow strip of land along the edge of a body of water separating it from other land areas; it is usually made up of any number of materials – sand, gravel, pebbles, cobbles, rock, or shells. These materials accumulate on the beach during periods of accretion or move away from the beach during periods of erosion. Beaches usually consist of tiny grains of rocks and minerals that have been worn down by constant pounding from the wind and waves. Some beaches are barrier beaches;

they protect inland ecosystems from harsh natural forces, such as hurricanes and storm surges. Beaches along river banks and river estuaries are different in appearance and habitat from those by the sea and ocean. Beaches are never stationary for long; constant changes due to wind, waves, tides, and human activities – including land management and recreation – continually alter the beach landscape. Beaches can be very different in appearance, for example, colour, size, and landscape. The appearance of a beach is mainly determined by the kind of rock or sand it is made of, having a variety of origins such as volcanic lava, high iron content red sand, or the white, bleached skeletons of millions of tiny corals. Fossil beaches can also be found all over the world; they are the remains of ancient seabeds that have been preserved due to a change in the sea level or a shift in elevation. The sand and stones that form the beach are created, transported, and influenced by the sea and the natural elements. Beaches can be hundreds of kilometres long or very short; they offer a very diverse habitat, and their often rapid change over the course of a few hours reveals different places and groups of living beings.

The biological zones of the sea

The *intertidal zone*, also known as the littoral zone, in marine aquatic environments is the area of the foreshore and seabed that is exposed to the air at low tide and submerged at high tide – the area between tide marks. In the intertidal zone the most common organisms are small and most are relatively uncomplicated creatures. This is for a variety of reasons. First, the supply of water that marine organisms require to survive in is intermittent. Second, the wave action around the shore can wash away or dislodge poorly suited or adapted organisms. Third, because of the intertidal zone's high exposure to the sun the temperature range can be extreme, from very hot to near freezing in frigid climates (with cold seas). Finally, the salinity is much higher in the intertidal zone because salt water trapped in rock pools evaporates leaving behind salt deposits. These four factors make the intertidal zone an extreme environment in which to live. A typical rocky shore can be divided into a splash zone (also known as the supra-tidal zone) – which is above the spring high-tide line and is covered by water only during storms – and an intertidal zone, which lies between the high and low tidal extremes. Along most shores, the intertidal zone can be clearly separated into the following subzones: high-tide zone, middle-tide zone, and low-tide zone.

The *high-tide zone* (or upper mid-littoral) is flooded during high tide only and is a highly saline environment. The abundance of water is not great enough to sustain large amounts of vegetation, although some do survive in the high-tide zone. The predominant organisms in this sub-region are anemones, barnacles, brittle stars, chitons, crabs, green algae, isopods, limpets, mussels, sea stars, snails, whelks, and some marine vegetation. The high-tide zone can also contain rock pools inhabited by small fish and larger seaweeds. Another organism found here is the hermit crab, which does extremely well because of its portable home (in the form of a shell). To an extent, this shell shelters the crab from the extreme temperature range and it can also carry water with it inside. Consequently there is generally a higher population of hermit crabs compared to common crabs in the high-tide zone. Life is much more abundant here than in the spray.

The *middle tide zone* is submerged and flooded for approximately equal periods of time per tide cycle. Consequently temperatures are less extreme due to shorter periods of direct exposure to the sun, therefore salinity is only marginally higher than ocean levels. However, wave action is generally more extreme than the high-tide and spray zones. The middle tide zone also has a much higher population of marine vegetation, specifically seaweeds. Organisms are also more complex and often larger in size than those found in the high-tide and splash zones. Organisms in this area include anemones, barnacles, chitons, crabs, green algae, isopods, limpets, mussels, sea lettuce, sea palms, sea stars, snails, sponges, and whelks. Again rock pools can also provide a habitat for small fish, shrimps, krill, sea urchins, and zooplankton. Apart from being more populated, life in the middle tide zone is more diversified than the high-tide and splash zones.

The *low tide zone* (or lower-littoral) sub-region is submerged for the majority of time, only being exposed for short periods at low tide, which provides a perfect habitat for organisms that are not well adapted to dryness and extreme temperatures. This area is teeming with life, having plenty of marine vegetation – unlike the other sub-regions – especially seaweeds, providing a haven for many creatures, including abalone, anemones, brown seaweed, chitons, crabs, green algae, hydroids, isopods, limpets, mussels, nudibranchs, sculpin, sea cucumber, sea lettuce, sea palms, sea stars, sea urchins, shrimp, snails, sponges, surf grass, tube worms, and whelks. The living creatures and marine vegetation of this sub-region grow larger than those in other zones due to the zone's shallow, light-filled, longer water-coverage, its lack of predators and the energy in its localised ecosystem. During the first Water School session we discovered we spent the most time in the unique low-tidal mudflats. They are extremely important ecosystems for migrating birds, such as sandpipers and plovers and visited by many people for the purpose of observing these birds.

The garden pond

> Wildlife gardening is not just valuable for nature – it's also great fun and incredibly fulfilling too. Square metre for square metre, Britain's gardens boast more biodiversity than any other habitat on the planet. So make your garden wildlife-friendly and then sit back and enjoy the fruits of your labours!
>
> (Moss, n.d.)

As unbelievable and unsuitable as it sounds, garden ponds can operate as a Water School site and are vital for nature conservation. Gardens cover a large area of land, far greater than nature reserves, protected areas, and other natural landscapes. They can provide a surprisingly large variety of habitats and they prove to be the key to survival for many varieties of wildlife. A typical suburban neighbourhood can offer a large and rich variety of ponds, shrubberies, and trees in neighbours' courtyards and gardens. When parts of the gardens are left natural, water and plants find their way to connect and together create an exciting network of small but important streams, canals, and embankments. Having some holes in boundary fencing at ground level enables animals to get in and out on their wanderings.

Gardens, regardless of their size, are very important from an educational point of view as they are easily accessible and are where children are most likely to enjoy wildlife. Through education, gardens can make a real difference, with important conservation activity carried out on the doorstep, linked to far greater ecological systems. Small ponds are really important for gardens; even tiny water features make a huge difference to the number and types of animals that visit a garden: they provide open water for drinking and bathing in dry weather conditions. Ponds develop really fast because many of the animals they create habitat for are highly mobile, therefore they attract birds, amphibians, insects, mammals, and a host of mini-beasts in a short period of time.

Ecology of a garden pond

Garden ponds have a unique ecology that needs careful management due to its size. As soon as a wildlife pond is built, it starts to fill up with plant life. This is a natural process known as 'succession'. To keep the pond for dragonflies, water beetles, and newts, the process of succession needs to be 'set back' over and over again. The surface and under the water can become too thick with vegetation very rapidly; pulling out excess growth will help to keep down algae. The life of a pond starts by being overtaken by a bloom of algae feeding frantically on the nitrogen in the water (from rain and tap water, and decaying plant matter), causing the pond to appear green. Eventually the tiny plants use all the food and fade away, leaving the stage set for slower-starting pond plants.

The depth profile of a pond is important, as the *deeper levels* allow hibernating amphibians (frogs, toads, and newts) and invertebrates (pond skaters, water boatmen, water beetles, and pond snails) to survive the coldest winters when the pond is frozen over. A *middle layer shelf* houses emergent plants and a gently sloping *shallow area* can be used by bathing birds, as it will warm up quickly in sunny weather and will be occupied by many invertebrates. A bog garden of wetland plants next to the pond will greatly increase the number of visitors to the pond. Densely planted, it will give cover to amphibians and invertebrates, and provide a new set of habitat species.

A bog garden or water garden is a moist or damp area around a pond that allows drainage. Naturally existing, lowland raised bog occurs in shallow basins or on flat, low-lying areas where poor drainage waterlogs the ground and slows down plant decay. Over thousands of years, layers of moss have developed into huge domes, rising up to ten metres above the landscape. These raised peat bogs are 98 per cent water (by weight) and occasionally form complexes where several domes can be found together, although each bog is distinct. Natural bog is fed entirely by rainwater – so is acidic – and supports a distinctive and unique range of wildlife. Undamaged natural bogs can have up to a dozen species of moss that support other plants such as common cotton-grass, cranberry, and bog rosemary. Sundews and bladderworts supplement their lack of nutrients by trapping and digesting unwitting insects. Some of the rarest insects – including the large heath butterfly, mire pill beetle, and several species of dragonfly – thrive in the wet conditions of raised bogs. Mossy hummocks and pools also provide vital nesting and feeding grounds for wading birds and birds of prey such merlins, which congregate on larger bogs to feed and roost during winter.

They are important water systems, storing and filtering water for slow release, providing a unique, living archive, storing a record of climate, vegetation, and landscape change since the last ice age.

While a pond contains standing water, the bog garden is just wet ground. Permanently damp, it creates an area where moisture-loving plants thrive, and being different from those suited to the standing water of a pond, it will create an extra habitat around the pond. A bog garden may be a better option than a pond for educating groups of very young children. As with a pond, it should also attract frogs and toads, possibly even grass snakes. Dragonflies and damselflies will perch on the taller grasses and other plants will attract bees and butterflies. This area will provide protection for many wildlife species as they leave the water, encouraging frogs to the area they will protect.

Native plants are spectacular, flowering from March to September, and encouraging their growth can support the fight against invasive aquatic species. There is a rather large variety of marginal (yellow flag iris, marsh marigold, water plantain, brooklime, ragged robin), emerging (greater spearwort, flowering rush, purple loosestrife), underwater (water soldier, water crowfoot, hornwort, ivy leaf duckweed, water-milfoil), and floating surface (fringed lily) plants to support nature. Submerged oxygenating plants – curly pondweed, for example – are the least beautiful plants, but vitally important in keeping the water clear and well oxygenated.

During the summer months a wildlife garden pond can attract dragonflies, damselflies, and mayflies. These creatures can spot a pond from high up in the air as it reflects the sunlight. Flying down, they meet with other water flies, mate, and lay their eggs either on the surface of the pond or in plant stems.

Park and garden ponds can provide a valuable link between people and wildlife. In the local park, village green, or school wildlife corner, ponds are a place to watch dragonflies, dip for tadpoles, or simply relax. The number of good wildlife ponds has declined due to changes in the way we manage our countryside and increasing pressures within our towns and cities. By creating new wildlife ponds we can help to reverse these declines. Wildlife ponds often support a small number of ducks and other water birds, but too many ducks will damage the wildlife value of a pond. Feeding ducks can be great fun and helps to bring children into contact with wildlife, however Water School provision helps children to learn that regular feeding will attract more birds than the pond can support; they can create disturbance and unused feed will sink to the bottom of the pond adding excessive nutrients and, as a result, the wildlife value of the pond declines.

Chapter 3

The pedagogy of Water School

Introduction

This chapter will outline the theoretical background of Water School education and will set out to define the pedagogical framework with its unique methods of teaching based on observation. The two main pillars of Water School pedagogy will be described: first, the philosophy or philosophical pedagogy, which is ultimately the way of thinking and beliefs related to the role and meaning of Water School education to educators and children; second, the methods of teaching, methodology, or practical pedagogy through which educators express their educational values and beliefs. The chapter will provide a set of unique tools that support practitioners in the delivery of the programme.

Pedagogy means the method and practice of teaching, that is, the study and the actual application or use of the idea and belief, trying to determine how best to teach. In terms of the Water School approach, the pedagogy aims to assist educators in the complete development of young children via the Water School programme, and to help practitioners and children with the imparting and acquisition of specific skills.

The philosophical pedagogy

The Water School approach is a type of outdoor education in which children regularly use natural forms of water – such as puddles, rain, and frost – to learn important life skills, including those existing as academic subjects of the educational curriculum, and to achieve a deep level of learning and development through individual interest, self-motivation, and reflection.

   The Water School programme is a nature education. It is the inspirational, partici-pant-focused, regular provision that offers participants the time and space to develop knowledge and self-growth through the natural qualities of water through physical and mental contact with the environment. The Water School programme uses the qualities of water – that have been observed by philosophers, theorists, and other scholars for centuries – as a means to build the children's psyche, together with physi-cal and emotional harmony, resulting in children's inner peace, which is necessary for future learning. The curriculum of Water School is built from cross-subject topics; the desired outcome of the curriculum is the development of children's high-level thinking and their understanding of complex natural processes, enabling them to be confident, motivated, and self-directed so they can accomplish individual learning in the outdoor classroom. The topics are all connected to natural forms of water, water's natural environment, the role of elements in nature, the complex working procedures of ecosystems, life supported by the wilderness, and recognition of specific living beings. The learning in this unique environment is not age- or ability-specific; it accommodates personal skill development and group learning. The natural environment and its elements are used to acquire knowledge about more abstract concepts that are directly linked to educational curriculum subjects, such as mathematics, physics, or biology.

The Water School philosophy is the fundamental nature of knowledge, reality, and existence within this educational approach. It also signifies the theory and attitude that acts as a guiding principle for the programme. Its philosophy is based on the feeling and passion of 'being in one's element'.

> We need to create environments – in our schools, in our workplaces, and in our public offices – where every person is inspired to grow creatively . . . We need to embrace the element . . . The features are aptitude and passion. The conditions are attitude and opportunity.
>
> (Robinson and Aronica, 2009, p. xiii, p. 21, p. 22)

Ken Robinson in his book, *The Element*, describes how the passion of being in the element can lead to peak performance. Ken Robinson argues that when people are in their element 'they connect with something fundamental to their sense of identity, purpose and well-being'. According to Robinson the element is where one's natural aptitudes meet one's personal passions. He believes that the quest for one's element is a two-way journey: an inward journey to explore the world within the self and an outward journey to explore the world around the self, trying to find ways of fitting in. The Water School programme prepares children for their own quest, teaches them to value the outcome, and helps them to find individual tools and techniques to do what it takes in life to achieve being in their element. The route to one's peak performance starts with the process of clarifying when one is in their individual element, for example describing favoured activities and reflecting on feelings when carrying out those activities. Once one's element is defined, one can focus more on being in their individual element. Peak performers do what they do best and often do it effortlessly, given the fact that carrying out the activity causes high levels of enjoyment and personal satisfaction. So by placing oneself in one's own element, motivates constant focusing and improving. Being in one's element nurtures the habit of self-development. In the Water School philosophy, the basic element is water, which has an innate relation to the human psyche; the direct relationship between being in water and becoming relaxed and happy has been observed for centuries by medical professionals and psychologists.

The ancient Greek philosopher Thales was born in Miletus in Greece (Internet Encyclopedia of Philosophy, n.d.). Aristotle, the major source for Thales' philosophy and science, identified Thales as the first person to investigate the basic principles, the question of the originating substances of matter and, therefore, as the founder of the school of natural philosophy. Aristotle laid out his own thinking about matter and form, which shed some light on the ideas of Thales, in *Metaphysics* (n.d.) Thales was interested in almost everything, investigating most areas of knowledge, philosophy, history, science, mathematics, engineering, geography, and politics. He proposed theories to explain many of the events of nature, the primary substance, the support of the earth, and the cause of change. Aristotle defined wisdom as knowledge of certain principles and causes. He commenced his investigation of the wisdom of the philosophers who preceded him with Thales. He recorded: 'Thales says that it is water'. 'It' is the nature, the archê, the originating principle. For Thales, this nature was a single material substance: water. Despite the more advanced terminology that Aristotle and Plato had created, Aristotle recorded the doctrines of Thales in terms that were available to Thales in the sixth century BCE. Thales' opinion that the earth rests on water is the most ancient explanation of natural processes. He explained his theory by adding the analogy that the earth is at rest because it is of the nature of wood and similar substances that have the capacity to float on water, although not on air. He explained that it floated because of a particular quality, a quality of buoyancy similar to that of wood. At the busy city-port of Miletus, Thales had unlimited opportunities to observe the arrival and departure of ships with their heavier-than-water loads, and recognised an analogy to floating logs. Thales's hypothesis was substantiated by sound observation and reasoned considerations. Thales believed that, because water was the permanent entity, the earth floats on water.

In the more modern understanding of Water School philosophy, being in one's element means any of the four substances (earth, air, fire, and water) that were once believed to constitute all physical matter on the earth. Any of these four substances were thought of as the natural environment for particular living beings. The natural or suitable environment – situation – for a person or thing, therefore, is what being in one's element really means.

The method and practice of teaching – via the unique qualities of natural water and the theoretical concepts it represents in nature – are forming the pedagogy of Water School. This pedagogy does not equal teaching. It is built from many different elements – elements meaning the first or basic principles – and covers the philosophical state, thinking process, and educational practice of the professionals who don't just teach, but accompany the young learners, care for them, and make their learning a life experience rather than simply schooling. The pedagogy of Water School celebrates balanced child-centred education that has set elements based on experiences offered by natural water and its environment.

The pedagogical thinking about teaching and education originates from many scholars, both historical and modern. Their heritage forms the important pillars of Water School pedagogy.

William Stearns Davis describes in his book *A Day in Old Athens: A Picture of Athenian Life* (Davis, 1960) that, in ancient Greek society, nurturing activities were divided between pedagogues and subject teachers. The first pedagogues were slaves who accompanied the children of their owners and sat beside them when being schooled. The expression itself originates from the Latin/Greek words *paid/paidos*, meaning boy, and *agogos*, meaning guide. Children were often put in their charge at around 7 years and remained with them until late adolescence. Plato talks about pedagogues as 'men who by age and experience are qualified to serve as both leaders (*hëgemonas*) and custodians (*paidagögous*)' of children (Longenecker, 1982: 53), the first being a companion, the second to help the young boys to learn what it was to be men. This they did by a combination of example, conversation, and discipline (Smith, 2012).

Nature provides balance of order and freedom. Educationalists who were advocates of nature education, like Pestalozzi, have expressed in their work their belief that education is rooted in human nature; it is a matter of head, hand, and heart. He believed that there should be a balance between learning through the child's own experience and the times when the teacher presents objects for study and then allows each child to use their senses for exploration (Frost, 2006). His combined strategy ensured meaningful introduction to concepts of the world for young children. Susan Sutherland Isaacs (as summarised by UK Essays, 2013) stated that one should respect the children's playtime, given that it is not an additional aspect of a child's life, because it is equal to the child's life. She opened the Malting House School in Cambridge in 1924 for highly advantaged children of professional parents. It was an experimental school with the aims: 'to stimulate the active enquiry of the children themselves rather than to teach them' and 'to bring within their immediate experience every range of fact to which their interests reached out' (Isaacs, 1930, cited in Tovey 2008:46). Children were given considerable freedom; Isaacs argued that 'play has the greatest value for the child when it is really free and his own' (Isaacs, 1929, cited in Tovey 2008:46). The garden had natural features (grass, trees, movable ladders, a flower and vegetable garden with individual plots for each child, and a range of animals). The garden motivated children to follow their curiosity and enquiry, while being ready to accept challenge and risk. Children had freedom to try things out, follow their passion, to investigate, to question, to experiment, and to follow wherever their curiosity led. The freedom provided, however, was freedom with constraints. For example children were allowed to climb on objects, but only one child at a time. The balanced approach brought educators closer to seeing the 'natural child'. Like Froebel and Montessori before her, Isaacs highlighted that freedom brought personal responsibility; this responsibility also empowered the children to develop skills to be safe. Margaret McMillan, also being a supporter of Froebel, believed outdoor play would improve a child's health. She built a terraced garden with apparatus for climbing and swinging, and included animals and birds in her garden. Children also helped grow community produce (UK Essays, 2013).

John Dewey (1963) understood play as 'a process of living and not a preparation for future living'. Good education for Dewey was dependent on the outdoor environment, given that is where life happens. He considered ordinary schools isolated from the real world, where children soak up knowledge and retain it for use when they are spontaneously induced to look into matters of compelling interest to themselves. They progress fastest in learning, not through being mechanically drilled in prefabricated material, but by doing work, experimenting with things, and changing them in purposive ways. Occasionally children need to be on their own, but in the main they will learn more by doing things together. By choosing what their group would like to do, by planning their work and helping each other to do it, trying out various ways and means of performing the tasks involved and discovering what will forward the project, then comparing and appraising the results, the youngsters would best develop their latent powers, their skills, understanding, self-reliance, and cooperative habits.

Froebel-trained Marjorie Allen was an enthusiastic advocate for children's rights and welfare throughout her lifetime and was principally responsible for introducing the concept of adventure playgrounds and planning for children's play from the child's point of view. She promoted the idea of 'junk' playgrounds and used scrap building materials as part of the play experience creating a place to pursue creative and imaginative play. During her travels Allen met Danish landscape architect, Carl Th. Sorenson, who had observed how much children enjoyed playing with 'loose parts', such as sticks, stones, boxes, ropes, and other open-ended play materials, more than the traditional playgrounds he had previously designed. In 1943 he built a new playground in Emdrup, Denmark, which he referred to as a 'junk playground', a place where children could naturally create and build whatever their imagination allowed.

Elements of the Water School approach

The Water School approach focuses on children being in their element. Building on historic views of childhood freedom and freedom of education, Water School uses the water and its natural appearance as the vehicle for the expression of freedom, based on the observation of:

- how orderly nature is;
- how water causes changes in short periods of time and how nature accepts the changes;
- how different the meaning of freedom is when in water and when being connected to natural water.

Freedom is an essential part of Water School education. One of the key factors that differentiate Water School from other outdoor education approaches is the type of freedom it offers. This freedom originates from the water and from its constantly moving natural forms. In this sense freedom and change are very closely related. There are many educational theorists who analyse freedom – both from its physical and psychological sense. In Water School education, freedom is a complex right that includes freedom of movement, thought, and activity. It also includes freedom of choice and respect toward the freedom of others, which – inevitably – includes order. First, when being in close proximity with water – being in the water – the body is in a different, almost contradictory, physical state. Limbs and fingers feel light but more difficult to move. Water is easy to manipulate but impossible to form. Children can contain it, but cannot keep it. When children are in water or playing with water, they are faced with a vast array of concepts that they are unlikely to experience elsewhere. These physical changes will directly affect the children's way of thinking; they often instantly become calm and observant and their exploration might develop to a whole new level. Even though many children encounter water play a couple of times a week, in its natural environment water offers much more: there are plants, animals, pebbles, and other materials within; it has different colours wherever one looks; it changes the size and appearance of objects underneath; and it constantly changes. It makes interesting sounds and represents different levels of speed. In Water School, as opposed to other outdoor approaches, the strong focus on the water – as both a medium for concepts to observe and the subject of the observation – motivates children to view change in a different light. Young children – whose cognitive skills develop through routine and repetition – are very sensitive to change. The element of surprise, rapid change, and the contradiction between the static objects underneath the fast layer of water inspire children's thinking and creativity.

While the basic element is water in its natural form, natural water itself is not the basis of the approach. The approach is a complex mixture of different things around water, a network of elements that connect to one another, forming the balanced teaching environment to accommodate unique teaching methods. The elements of the approach are: play, adults, environment, special experiences, time, materials, individual learning styles, and imitation.

Play in its organic form is the life of children. It cannot be described simply as activities, skills, attitude, or learning. Play is the life of the child – the means of being, existing, expression, and connection.

Adults working with children become part of the environment as resources: the environment is a child's first experience of real life, and adults in it are the field-study subjects of a child's emotional imitation and projection. This imitation and projection creates the basis of the child's later development, a framework for all emotional, social, and communication processes.

The *environment*, as an element of Water School, operates as the orderly, safe, but still risky and surprising framework for children's creativity. Water in the environment is a constant feature that provides the familiar and the unknown in this approach.

Time is a key element of the approach that carries different – almost contradictory – layers of meaning. Time becomes unimportant; however, allowing time is of great significance and value. Time perception outdoors means the subjective experience of time, which is measured by someone's own perception of the duration between two events. Another person's perception of time cannot be directly experienced or understood; therefore environments that accommodate the personal perception of time are extremely important for the developing mind.

Natural materials also have real significance for children. A wide range of natural objects can be used as open-ended tools for exploration and imagination, which stimulate all of the senses and deep-level thinking. Natural materials provide a good range of textures, temperatures, and shapes and together with natural loose parts – natural materials that can be freely picked up, such as fallen leaves, pieces of driftwood, pebbles – afford an array of open-ended learning processes, such as building, sorting, counting, and dramatic play. These materials are available all year round and have a perfectly imperfect beauty that inspires children's creativity and thinking processes.

Children own characteristics and individual learning style is another main element of the Water School approach and its learning process. Children's perception of the world and the way they sense the environment is greatly affected by their individual ways of understanding. Children make sense of the environment based on their past and immediate experiences. In their early years children are mainly sensory learners, meaning information is received and processed based on senses. An early appreciation of a child's preferential learning style can help adults to encourage them to learn in different environments and situations. Being aware of an adult's own learning style – that might conflict with the children's preferred style – will support effective teaching. The individual learning styles in Water School are the ways in which children experience the water and its environment. This ultimately leads to the outcome of Water School education: how children make sense of the experience and what they consider as important within it.

The role of elements in Water School

The role of play

> A play experience is therapeutic because it provides a secure relationship between the child and the adult, so that the child has the freedom and room to state himself in his own terms, exactly as he is at the moment in his own way and in his own time.
>
> (Axline, 1950)

During the history of humanity a large number of childhood education and health professionals have observed that play is an important factor when it comes to human happiness and well-being. Play is a fun, enjoyable activity, which elevates the human spirit and brightens the view of life. It expands self-expression, self-knowledge, self-motivation, and self-reflection. Play relieves feelings of anxiety and helplessness; connects people in a naturally desired way; stimulates deep thinking, creativity, and investigation; regulates human emotions; and develops emotional intelligence, while creating a safe framework for practising life skills and social models needed for healthy development. In play, children gain and discharge energy, prepare for life's duties, achieve confidence, and release negative feelings. When children play, they learn to express their inner thoughts and the individuality of their personalities, and learn to develop their sense of self. Creativity begins through the creative process of play where children bring objects and concepts to life, recreate their environmental experiences, and communicate their understanding through the use of metaphors.

Water as a part of play often has cleansing symbolism. Water is one of most popular unstructured play mediums for young children. It is simple to manipulate, and with its unique characteristics water can symbolise just about anything in play. Water allows children to act out extreme feelings without serious consequences, without hurt or a permanent effect. Water is a reversible play material, and – especially in its natural appearance and environment – it allows transparency and mystery. Children can easily succeed and experience satisfaction as there is no prescribed, right or wrong way to play with water.

In this organic play process, water is children's vocabulary and play is the actual communication. Play in Water School is not child's play in its common meaning. Play is the means and method of connection. It is the way children connect to all of the elements: adults, environment, materials, experiences, and the self. Children play to connect links; this is what their brain is programmed to do (classically known as the wiring of the brain). Water School provides children with a medium, a platform that allows the connection to happen naturally.

Play from the child's point of view should, however, mainly be undertaken as an activity for joy and well-being – even though it isn't always light-hearted, deep concentration is often required – with the added purpose of assisting learning and development. The purpose of play as a connection should occur naturally and unconsciously, without the child realising its educational nature. It is the role of the adults to facilitate and provide an environment that ensures and supports play as a natural process. In Water School, the qualities of the environment are provided naturally, allowing the adults to focus on the children's needs and expression, rather than planning the environment.

The role of adults

In classic education the adults around young children are typically understood as educators who deliver a concrete curriculum following a pre-determined programme. They are usually committed to their preferred methods of delivery, influenced by their own experiences of education.

In Water School, however, the role of adults has many different layers and the importance of the layers is constantly changing, depending on the other key elements – mainly the learning styles, the environment, and the materials. As the environment of Water School – and the water within – is a complex, accomplished vehicle for play and learning, the adults' role that enables their role to contain the children's play process is equally complex.

The adult as provocateur

Provocation, as it is understood in the Reggio Emilia approach, means an enquiry or discovery activity that is an arranged situation in the children's environment, set up by the adult to encourage children's thought processes. In Water School, however, given the rapidly changing environment, the water-based experiences set the provocations naturally. The adults' roles as provocateurs change, transform, and expand. The adult as provocateur will become a pointer/guide/showcase producer, as the main role of the provocateur will be to point the children into the direction of the natural provocation.

The adult as follower

Once the natural provocation has occurred the adult needs to become a follower, following the children as they set out to walk over their route of discovery introduced by the natural provocation. Following the children is accomplished by respecting young children's right to explore, discover, and shape their individual learning. Following the lead of the children focuses on child-initiated learning, not relying on just being there by chance, although adults will highlight opportunities within the natural environments enriched with materials that are developmentally and individually appropriate. Many of the activities that children engage in should be child-initiated rather than teacher-directed. In Water School children are naturally offered meaningful choices by the environment itself, therefore it is natural for adults to follow rather than direct.

The adult as facilitator

Becoming an active participant in children's learning through meaningful interactions and taking part in their play helps the adult become an informed decision-maker, therefore acquiring the knowledge to become an excellent facilitator. Once adults experience what is happening in children's play through engagement, adults can then be instructors and facilitators. A facilitating adult guides the children into a safe and accepting environment that places as few limits as possible on the child, enabling them to express themselves in a way that suits them. The facilitator aims to build a trusting relationship with the children and, via the relationship, interacts with them in their play. The facilitator enables the safe place by containing and holding children's experiences and feelings in order to help them make sense of their world. Facilitating the environment in Water School means giving the children the chance to explore the environment and allowing the responsibility of choosing how to spend their time, while still being more directive if needed.

Facilitating in this way originates from the Project Approach (Sargent, 2011), which builds on natural curiosity, facilitating the environment and situations where children can interact, question, connect, problem-solve, communicate, reflect, and more. This kind of authentic learning extends beyond the classroom to each student's home, community, nation, and the world. It essentially makes learning the stuff of real life and children active participants in and shapers of their worlds.

The adult as narrator

The narrator is generally a person who recounts the events that happen, often, in real time. A narrator refers to the sequence of events and is crucial for the way an event is perceived by its audience. Adults in educational settings usually give different types of narrative. Gérard Genette, a French literary theorist, refers to narrators as homodiegetic and heterodiegetic (1982). A homodiegetic narrator describes his or her own personal experiences as a character in the story. Such a narrator cannot know more about other characters than what their actions reveal. A heterodiegetic narrator, in contrast, describes the experiences of the characters that appear in the story. In 'stories' in an educational setting, the author may also be omniscient and employ multiple points of view and comment on events as they occur.

The narrator is a fair and non-directive adult who is part of the process, providing the interpretation of the material that arises during a session, giving an insight to the children's internal world, interpreting and analysing the children's thoughts and feelings and reflecting it back to the child. The role of an adult narrator in Water School is to add interesting information about the environment in relation to the children's personal experiences.

The adult as mentor, responder, and guide

The adult role is to observe children, listen to their questions and their stories, find out what interests them, and then provide them with opportunities to explore these interests further. This means that projects aren't planned in advance, they emerge based on the child's interests, therefore the adults mentor children and guide them on their chosen routes. The mentor adult will offer the children a reflective narrative and constructive feedback. A good mentor knows this and will deliver feedback in a way that will help the children gain insight to further develop specific qualities or skills. As a guide, the adults need to be able to define when the children are in need of guidance. Giving unwelcome feedback can be detrimental to anyone who is not ready to accept the it; good feedback should explain, show, and share rather than tell. A good mentor is reliable, trustworthy – not opinionated – and confidential. An adult as a mentor minimises assumptions and prejudices. A good mentor gives advice without constraints or direct expectations. First and foremost, as a mentor/guide the adults need to direct children in a way that guarantees a degree of success, highlighting and celebrating any achievements they may accomplish. The aim of a good adult mentor is to help build children's confidence, resulting in a high level of independence.

The guiding role of the adult is very effective when children enter unknown places where they need gentle guidance in navigating themselves through the experience.

The adult as a visitor, observer

The children's learning processes and activities should be seen as one-time, exciting attractions, places that adults are privileged to visit. For its value, meaning, and beauty, children's learning should be respected and admired by adults when they are allowed by the children to spend time or stay with them. Children – as organisers and owners of the events – will determine the exact rights of the visitors. Adults, as visitors of learning, will befriend children and take an interest in each individual child, offering support and a listening ear. As long-term or regular visitors, adults need to try building a long-term relationship, establishing continuity and stability.

Children, themselves, often become quiet onlookers in Water School. As they innately connect with water in its natural form and environment, children often quieten down; in order to witness their experience, engagement, and learning process – without missing important and unique details – adults need to develop a silent observer role.

The adult as listener, audience

The adult as the listener is a less active role. It differs from being an observer, as the adult as listener may not demonstrate any relationship with the child, but is 'only' a positive witness. The listener will be present with interested eye contact and with facial expressions but will let the child become an active learner; the children can then fulfil their own dreams, tasks, and responsibilities as researchers and constructors of their own knowledge. This role of listening is, however, not passive, as having a good listener teaches children how to become better listeners themselves. Listening is an important part of communication; listening does not equal hearing. Being a good and patient listener helps children to solve many of life's problems in the future and it helps them to see the world through the eyes of their peers. Adult benefits greatly from this role, as it enriches the understanding of the children and expands the capacity for empathy for both the listener's and the presenter's side.

In Water School, the active listener is similar to the observer audience; however, it means the children make a direct connection with the adult (looking at them or talking to them) and the adults need to respect their input and choose sensitively how to interact without speaking or giving ready answers. Children's narratives of the events or the verbal expression of their thoughts is often 'only' a part of their inner process, which they say out loud simply as means of expression, without expecting a verbal response.

The adult as interviewer

Open-ended questions have a major role in keeping a child focused, interested, and motivated during an activity, opening new perspectives and setting new directions for children. Open-ended questions encourage children to use language and give fuller answers that draw on a wider range of their knowledge and vocabulary, while having to use actively built complete sentences. The open-ended questions motivate children to think about their answers and give details to really answer the question and elaborate with details, while expressing their own thoughts and opinions. While answering open-ended questions children need to use their creativity, think of new ideas, and use their imagination to solve problems. In the long term this will aid their cognitive development and help them to build relationships as they become more involved in the conversations. Children are able to relate something of meaning, and respond to the person/people with whom they are communicating. In this way, open-ended questions will be used positively to build and deepen relationships. When children are asked open-ended questions, adults show them that their opinions, ideas, thoughts, and feelings matter and it tells a child that their contribution is important. Open-ended questions strengthen children's positive self-esteem and self-image, as well as strengthening the relationship between the adult and the children.

Open-ended questions are significant in the Water School learning process. As children engage and start to be in their element, their inner thought process unfolds. The adult becomes an interviewer when children appear to be stuck in their inner thought process, and by gently offering a different perspective via open-ended questions, the adults gain a better understanding of how the child relates to the water, the environment, and the experience.

The adult as note taker, recorder

The adult as a recorder will place an emphasis on carefully documenting children's thoughts, ideas, and progression of thinking, making their inner thought process visible in many different ways: photographs, transcripts of children's thoughts and explanations, visual representations (drawings, sculptures etc.) are all designed to show the child's learning process. The adult as a 'documentalist' focuses intensively on recording children's personal experiences and memories in a variety of ways. Documentation typically includes samples of children's work at different stages, with comments by note-taker adults based on their discussions with the children, to create an exact picture of the children's participation, interests, and development, helping adults to engage with their roles in the children's learning.

The Water School programme – given its unique environment and characteristics – needs special methods of observation that follow children's process, rather than documenting the obvious. Using the special Water School observation methods, children become partner-observers of their own learning.

The adult as companion, co-learner, and collaborator

The role of adults as co-learners means simply working together on projects and becoming personally engaged in the process as it evolves. The children learn about the world and the adults learn about the children. The adult as a co-learner respects that children construct their own understanding of concepts, therefore their insight and interpretation can provide the co-learning adult with a new understanding. As the children constantly draw on each other for inspiration, guidance, and help, becoming a co-learner will provide the adult with a new take on the children as a group, and the individual child. When the adult appears as a co-learner, their instruction/guidance is likely to be better received by the children, as the adults are likely to deliver instructions as meaningful options rather than demands.

In Water School the role of the adults as companions strongly supports the adults in fulfilling the other roles. All people have an innate relationship with water; however, the level of the engagement might be different. Through understanding their own thought processes, adults have a far greater ability to understand children.

The adult as police

The policing role of the adult also covers the delivery of limits. Setting and enforcing limits is an important part of parenting and education. Play therapists state: 'a child without limits is an abused child. Without limits there is no sense of safety, boundaries or protection in the world. Children without limits cannot trust adults to behave in a consistent manner' (Barnes, 2001). The limits should be planned and constructed from loving interest in and concern for a child, not for a desire for power over the child. The children should, however, have as few limits as possible.

In the Water School programme, limitations are based on health and safety and the protection of the environment. To achieve children 'being on board', adults as police need to allow the children to become the part of the 'force'. Assessing risks – together with the children – is an important part of the Water School approach, especially given the fact that there should be minimal restriction. Yet there is a high-risk resource: the water at the centre of the education.

The role of the environment

The environment in today's early childhood education is highly appreciated for its effect on children's development. The different types of environment that children enter and in which they learn to exist are categorised in different ways, based on attributes, qualities, size, location, purpose, or origin, and they are all observed to have negative or positive effects on the growing mind.

In the Water School approach the role of environment is to facilitate the children's relationship with nature. The way this relationship forms is based on the experiences young children have with nature. Children sense and receive nature experiences differently, but its reception is mainly directed by the environment itself. Nature experiences can be grouped in three different categories:

1   close, personal, and physical
2   distant, programmed, and physical
3   emblematic and mental.

The close, personal experience of nature occurs when children spend time in nature. During these experiences children can witness nature's sustainable, mainly self-directed, features in their natural forms, including plants and animals, natural and often living resources where they enjoy freedom in its classic sense. This experience is physical; children can be contained within the environment, can smell, touch, see, hear, and even taste. In many early years educational settings, this includes going to the park or visiting a local pond or stream.

The distant, programmed experience can still include close proximity to natural features such as animals and plants but the experience that occurs is a highly controlled, human-built, and human-managed environment where the activities and choices are pre-planned and limited. This type of experience is planned and framed, with qualities of natural wildness and features of the natural world but in a more domesticated way. These tend to include gardening, pet keeping and visits to local farms, nature reserves, museums, or zoos. This kind of encounter with nature is distant – not physically but mentally. The distant nature of the experience indicates that, although children have a physical contact with nature, they cannot emerge in it through their senses, cannot become contained within the environment, therefore the experience is significantly different and somewhat limited.

The emblematic experience means that children, rather than being in nature or meeting living organisms, encounter things (places, resources etc.) that serve as symbols of the particular qualities or concepts of nature education. The emblematic experience includes looking at books, photos, listening to stories, watching movies or cartoons, attending art exhibitions, listening to CDs of natural sounds or music, and working with natural resources incorporated into everyday learning activities.

Many educational theories explore how nature can be incorporated into children's learning, even in less nature-rich places. The theory of 'loose parts' was first proposed by architect Simon Nicholson in the 1970s. Nicholson observed that the 'loose parts' in the environment empower human thinking and creativity. This began to influence the child-play experts, who design play spaces for children.

The simple facts are these:

1   There is no evidence, except in special cases of mental disability, that some young babies are born creative and inventive, and others not.

2   There is evidence that all children love to interact with variables, such as materials and shapes; smells and other physical phenomena, such as electricity, magnetism and gravity; media such as gases and fluids; sounds, music, motion; chemical interactions, cooking and fire; and other humans, and animals, plants, words, concepts and ideas. With all these things all children love to play, experiment, discover and invent and have fun.

(Nicholson, 1972)

In children's play this means resources and materials that can be transported, mixed, taken, shifted, incorporated, mingled, arranged, disassembled, and assembled in a large variety of ways. These materials have no unique, correct, or incorrect way to be used. Natural loose parts in a preschool children's environment can include an array of materials for use in play such as stones, stumps, sand, gravel, twigs, wood, plants, flowers, baskets, logs, stones, flowers, sand, shells, mud, rocks, leaves, mown grass, and seeds. Having 'loose parts' available in a play space allows children to use the materials as they choose or are motivated toward. Children often prefer to play with materials that they can use freely and adapt as they would like. Encouraging children to use resources creatively and individually can provide a wider range of opportunities than adult-led activities. Children playing with loose parts are using their imagination and developing more skills and competence than they would playing with 'defined usage' toys.

In the Water School environment, especially when surrounded with water, the play materials and areas are all purposeful and open-ended. This environment places a special focus on the type of intervention the adults need to provide, as their responsibility is not teaching, testing, or challenging but supporting and encouraging children in the challenging environment, so they can gain sufficient knowledge to follow their own ideas. 'Loose parts' theory in the Water School environment basically means the best play comes from items that allow children to express their line of thought in many different ways and on many different levels. Water School environments, with its 'loose parts', is naturally more stimulating and engaging than static environments; one of its unique characteristics is the showcase of rapid, short-term changes that happen in front of the children's eyes. This kind of play environment promotes development opportunities that do not direct play, but allow children to develop their own ideas and explore their world in their own preferred way.

The Process of Nature Encounter

Children respond to nature in an extremely active manner, especially in its natural forms, which act as high-intensity stimuli, touching all senses. They do not just see, but sense, accept, appreciate, understand, and react to nature. Through this process – The Process of Nature Encounter – children's first natural awareness progresses into research. When changes happen in nature and the children progress from one stage to the next, the process speeds up and this stimulates the children to learn even more, to seek newer and newer experiences.

- *Sensing*: in this stage children develop an awareness of the natural environment and start to sense the world around them.
- *Accepting*: in this stage children – with their awareness of the environment – become open to accepting the impulses and stimuli coming from their direct relationship to nature.
- *Appreciating*: in this stage children become interested and don't just accept the experiences but seek out the opportunities to encounter them.
- *Understanding*: in this stage children internalise their experiences and develop their own individual opinions, likes and dislikes, memories, and knowledge.
- *Re-acting and reacting*: in this stage children develop their capacity to use their knowledge to influence their actions in the natural environment.

Tim Gill, one of the UK's leading commentators on childhood, expands on the significance of this: 'Natural places are singularly engaging, stimulating, life-enhancing environments where children can reach new depths of understanding about themselves, their abilities and their relationship with the world around them' (Gill, 2009).

The role of the special experiences: senses

Young children are mainly sensory motor learners. When newly born, babies have a well-developed sense of touch overall but a limited finger pad sensitivity, and – due to nature's programmed survival instinct – the majority of their senses are concentrated around certain areas on their bodies, for example their lips. To aid young children's development, adults need to ensure a sensory-rich environment with many textures, temperatures, colours, smells, and sounds. Nature and the great outdoors is an ideal learning environment for children as all their senses are stimulated by the rich source of sensory experiences.

Their physical development is also advancing to new levels as, in response to the many different sources of stimuli, the varied environment motivates children to move their bodies in many different ways. Being outdoors also supports children, as natural physical aids (such as sitting between logs) will help children to concentrate on other activities, rather than the movements themselves. The outdoor environment has a great impact on the development of vision, hearing, and touch of children too. In the outdoor environment their brain, motivated by the stimuli, builds new neural pathways – known as the wiring of the brain – in response to the demand of coping with the vast array of new information.

As babies interact with their widening world, in the absence of language to describe what they encounter, the information processing is motivated, decoded, and understood by their senses. Babies' sight and ability to use other senses is limited at first, but the abilities of young minds become wider and deeper, as they experience more and more. Their awareness can be heightened and improved more quickly in Water School, as their senses are challenged and stimulated by a larger variety of textures, visual images, sounds, and smells. While babies have no words to engage with others about their impressions, thoughts, and feelings, Water School provides many opportunities for the educators to use descriptive language effectively to develop babies' understanding of the surroundings and their own responses to their environment. For example:

- touch – I am pouring water on you. Can you feel the cold and wet water?
- sight – Do you see the fish in the water?
- hearing – Can you hear the dripping water?
- smell – Look at that yellow flower. Would you like to smell this flower?

Using the language will solidify the meanings of words and help babies to make sense of their world. In Water School, babies' limited mobility and dexterity does not affect their ability to interact with the world, as the environment offers a lot of possibilities in a small space, starting from something as simple as placing a baby on the grass near the water. Babies can enjoy the feeling of water, take in the movement of wind, and respond to the sounds of birds. Feeling a variety of materials, touching small objects, and experimenting with the properties of cause and effect will impact their brain activity positively. However, despite the large variety of impulses, the natural environment is unlikely to cause a stimulation overload due to its genuinely balanced movements, coordinating colours, and spontaneously existing rhythm. Babies' interior stimulation signals and the outer sensory signals in the Water School environment seem to be harmonised to achieve a calming effect.

One of the magical qualities of the Water School experience is that all the activities that would need careful planning and organisation indoors in order to offer a sufficiently rich, nurturing, and appropriately challenging environment for very young children, occur naturally, stimulating children's senses: hearing, vision, smell, touch, spatial awareness, physical freedom, and sense of belonging.

Sound moves in a different way outdoors – for example, on large beaches; due to the lack of physical limits and the effects of natural forces, sound changes naturally with the wind or variations in air pressure. In the very early stages of development children are able to differentiate sounds much more effectively than adults, therefore they're significantly more receptive to air movement and animal sounds. Young children are also naturally programmed to be curious and alert, and as a result they love being outdoors, especially around the sound of water.

Light also has different effects in an outdoor environment with water features. Sometimes it is changed very rapidly by the weather – even in as little as 15 minutes. In a Water School environment light is filtered by vegetation, water, and landscape features, and changes significantly throughout different parts of the site. Light effects in natural water features act as a great source of fascination. The changes in light stimulate the eyes to adapt, which then stimulates the brain.

Smell is also greatly influenced and stimulated outdoors. Different smells (such as grass, earth, flowers, rain, mud etc.) that children are unlikely to encounter in a conventional outdoor setting encourage them to investigate the source of the smell. The different sources of smells are naturally occurring at different levels and locations so children need to work out how to access them. Young children, as they grow and develop, move rapidly from a warm, soft, protective environment to a different world with many different sensations. Children take time to get used to these feelings and they learn about life with each touch – touch being the key sense for helping them to learn. In the Water School environment children can feel textural differences more effectively – it can offer a sensory wonderland like no other.

Children appreciate the liveliness and colours of the Water School environment, but not necessarily the stereotypical choices of adults. Warmer natural tones, softer tones rather than brash, bold colours can help the child develop a sense of refined appreciation, and they like the splashes of brighter tones that can be found in nature. Children are very sensitive to the flow of energy and the relation of external objects, which helps the growing brain to understand location and integration in a larger sense; the Water School environment provides this naturally. Children like natural places as they are creative, active, reflective, emotional, and social. Through the understanding of natural processes children will find their place in their surroundings and develop a sense of space, a sense of belonging.

The role of time

> The universe is full of magical things, patiently waiting for our wits to grow sharper.
> (Phillpotts, 1919)

Time is an integral part of daily life, but it is omnipresent and immaterial. It is important for young children to understand, but as opposed to other senses that are stimulated and coordinated by specialised sensory receptors, there is no specific receptor for time. Children start life with a false concept of time: it is hard for them to realise the difference between day and night: they live in 'now'.

To develop a real understanding of time children need to understand the relationship between events in their surroundings, which they understand through an internal coordination based on observation (Kamii and Russell, 2010). According to Piaget (1927/71) children develop a sense of time as two separate concepts: physical and psychological time – a difference between the actual passing minutes and hours and a more personalised, individual feeling of time. While understanding time, children develop an awareness of duration, simultaneity, reversibility, and succession. This means an ability to make sense of events in the past, present, and future; to recognise the order in which events occur; to understand the lengths of an activity in relation to another; and to accept that things can happen together.

Very young children 'live in time' before gaining an awareness of the fact that time actually passes by. They are unable to estimate time correctly unless they are made to pay attention to it, experiencing time in terms of how long it takes to do something. The awareness of time improves during childhood as children's attention and short-term memory capacities develop a process dependent on the slow maturation of the prefrontal cortex. At the age of five or six, children are able to sense continuum based on having learnt to associate durations with particular actions. Children's perception of time changes with their development, but – very importantly – research has shown (Droit-Volet et al., 2011; Rudd et al., 2012) that it is affected by a person's emotional state.

Perception of emotions has the ability to change the sense of time. For example, spending time with particular activities or people or listening to something can adversely affect one's internal clock. Recent research (Rudd et al., 2012) has found that the feeling of awe has the ability to expand one's perception of time availability. Awe can be characterised as an experience of immense perceptual vastness that coincides with an increase in focus. Consequently, it is conceivable that one's temporal perception would slow down when experiencing awe. Rudd et al. (2012) summarised, based on their experiments, that being in the present moment elongates time perception, and experiencing the wonder of the moment caused people to perceive that they had more time available and lessened their impatience and boosted their satisfaction, having a direct implication on people's opinion on how they spent their time. Similarly, many other researchers have observed that feelings have a direct effect on time perception and vice versa. Menzies (2005) stated that people report feeling a toll on well-being when feeling time starved.

The Water School environment is the ideal place to nurture children's sense of awe and, therefore, perception of time.

The role of Water School materials

Readily available but often underrated materials have a significant role in the Water School programme due to their unique characteristics that distinguish them from the usual play resources. The following materials can be found in all the different Water School sites: *mud, sticks, rocks/pebbles, natural forces, light,* and *water.*

Mud

Children have been playing in dirt and earth throughout human history. Views and approaches about using mud with children have formed and transformed as centuries and circumstances changed, but one thing has remained stable: children simply love mud. Mud is an underrated but creative and versatile material with the exceptional qualities of being cheap, accessible, and open-ended. Mud has been used for a variety of purposes throughout history, from building to beauty, through to playing, healing, and making art. With educators' changing attitude toward nature and sustainability, mud certainly re-gained its validity and value as an educational resource. Mud connects children with nature, which cannot be replaced by technology; there is a direct psychological effect and immediate environmental awareness. It has a distinctive, relaxing smell and texture. There is an innate biological connection between humans and the natural environment that evolved by being in the natural environment for millennia. Mud can make people happier and healthier.

Research lead by Chris Lowry and his colleagues at University of Bristol has shown that playing in dirt and very wet mud improves children's immune systems (Lowry *et al.*, 2007) Earth and natural dirt contains a harmless, microscopic soil bacterium (called Mycobacterium vaccae) that increases the levels of serotonin in the brain, helping soothe, calm and improve cognitive function. During the research, participants being exposed to the bacteria reported increased vitality and decreased pain. Being a sensory activity, and with its direct effects on the brain, playing in mud develops children intellectually. It encourages creative, shared thinking and accommodates social relationships. It meets the needs and levels of children in different developmental stages and all age groups can gain from the activity. It is a wonderful art medium and responds in a variety of ways when combined with other materials and media. As an experience, mud is the perfect material for complex learning. It is mouldable, but dries hard; it can be used dry and wet; it is perfect on its own but can be mixed with other materials; and above all, mud permits mistakes and still guarantees success. Children can enhance their skills, practise their communication and maths by talking, measuring, weighing, constructing, creating, shaping, decorating, examining, and sharing. For these reasons, mud is inviting, challenging, exciting, and appropriate. As soon as children start to play in the mud, they begin to mould and shape it. They become aware that they are in charge and have influence over the medium as it immediately responds to their touch. The feeling that they are in charge of the material, provides the confidence to attempt other learning curves, which opens the door to greater self-expression and imagination. Mud also allows children to learn to repair mistakes and not be afraid to make them. Making mistakes is essential for self-improvement but can be difficult and even an obstacle for some children.

Sticks

Natural resources – especially sticks – are probably the world's oldest toys; even animals play with sticks. Almost any child will find sticks an endless source of pretending and fun. Sticks can turn into magic fairy wands, bows and arrows, kindling for a fire, or building material. When children incorporate sticks into their play, they plan, they solve problems, they share and manipulate, and their creativity and imagination develops effortlessly. They discover the surrounding natural environment as they try to find the required stick for the defined purpose, and as they act, their acts gain meaning and real successes emerge. Children engage in sports with sticks, they create, they tell stories and remember. Sticks are original building blocks for developmental play, both physically and mentally. Sticks, being completely open ended, promote meaningful free play – the freedom to explore, invent, try, study, and correct – without the need for prior planning. Coming in different sizes, weights, lengths, shapes, and forms sticks encourage even the shyest of children to look around. Sticks are all over the world, they are natural, sustainable, and free. Nothing proves more the versatile nature of sticks than the fact that artists, craft professionals, designers, and even architects find use for them in masterpieces, baskets, household items, and buildings. Playing with sticks is an irresistible activity for children and grown-ups, from fishing with a rod, through to drawing with a pen and using a wooden spoon, this all derives from the same original roots. Despite the changed physical, social, cultural, economic, and political landscape, using sticks children of today can still have the complex, innate connection to the natural world that is biologically driven and instinctively determined.

Rocks and pebbles

When young children are learning about the world they live in, humble rocks and pebbles (as loose parts) are truly worthy of attention. One of the advantages of rocks and pebbles is that they can be found just about anywhere and can be used for anything a child can imagine. They can be food in a play kitchen or products in a shop; they can be transported, transformed, and hidden. They can be mixed with other materials, and to our young children they can be a versatile, constant source of engagement. They can be gathered, arranged, sorted, compared, or even crushed. As teaching materials, rocks and pebbles can provide physical activity, teamwork, problem-solving tasks, shared experience, co-operation, experimentation, imagination, creativity, literacy, and numeracy.

Natural forces

The idea of approaching the topic of natural forces as a teaching resource in early years might seem wild for some. Ultimately, it is indeed fun to be outdoors and feel that one's body, limbs, movements, and voice are part of the natural elements. It certainly takes thinking outside the box, but whatever activity practitioners offer indoors can be completed outdoors, and the chances are great that the learning will be deeper, more involved, and definitely long-term. The benefits of teaching children to perceive natural forces as adventure are vast. Changes of nature, surfaces, landscapes, colours, and shapes offer a wide range of resources to explain and demonstrate basic concepts that need to be understood in many learning and development areas. Children learn great adaptation and life skills: investigation and questioning, patience, and problem-solving; they learn about their own bodies, their health and limitations; children can learn to be to be prepared, to be self-reliant, and to explore their immediate and larger environment. By experiencing the sensory stimulation offered when encountering natural forces – especially in the event of weather change – children will gain a fuller body awareness and spatial awareness. By approaching nature at the time of change children will learn about risk and gain a respectful connection to nature that is one of the main factors in sustainability and the future of planet Earth: learning about how flora and fauna grows, understanding pollution and its environmental effects, learning about the cycle of ecology system, and how to care for and preserve nature and its habitats.

Having a positive attitude toward being outdoors whatever the weather and being part of the environment will reduce the environmental stress that affects children through television, computers, and other electronic media. When children are outdoors in a changing environment their ability to create social bonds is significantly greater with friends and family and makes a great conversation starter for language and conversational skills. They are also less worried about personal possessions and having to share. Snow, rain, and wind play requires creativity, scientific observation, and negotiation skills and the social skills to communicate their ideas. There is a great amount of creativity and imagination fostered as children build snow and wet-mud creatures, and as they use various objects to decorate them. They have to work as a team to overcome barriers and they have to accept and share failure and success. Experiencing changes in nature will enable children to accept changes in their own body size and control over the movements of their body. Outdoors, extreme conditions allow children to achieve milestones at different rates, so they are likely be accomplished in each child's individual way. Educators will be able to support development more successfully by providing appropriate experiences based on the individual progress of each child.

Light

> Night transforms the natural world into a very different place; for some children it is a time of excitement and discovery, but for others it is sinister and frightening. Yet darkness itself is not something to be fearful of, and the more the children find out about the mysteries of night the less scary they will seem.
>
> (Danks and Schofield, 2005)

Experiencing light and dark in a natural environment – especially with reflections created by water – provides magical moments that children will thoroughly enjoy and learn from. Light and darkness have true natural fascination, awe, and wonder and their mysterious quality carries an element of risk and challenge and an opportunity for young children to experience facing their fears and worries in a safe frame. Natural changes of light and darkness greatly motivate children's curiosity and allow them to engage in sustained shared thinking and open discussion, where the issues occur in front of their eyes. Locations with natural water are wonderful for exploring the magic of light and dark, the mystery of shadows, the changes of the sun and the sky – all supporting the world of imagination and endless possibilities in which the children prefer to learn.

Water

It has been suggested that our connections with water are hard-wired into our genetic makeup (Deakin University and Parks Victoria, 2002) as a survival mechanism from our hunter-gatherer days. Therefore, children reared apart from nature are necessarily limited (Rivkin, 1995: 6). As a natural material, water appeals to children of all ages. Play in water's natural environments is thought to have restorative properties; it alleviates stress and helps to regulate thoughts, feelings, reactions, and emotions. The original kinds of water-fun – jumping in streams, pond dipping, rain splashing – seem to help children to play more co-operatively: once building bridges over streams, children tend to forget their differences.

Natural water has many features that conventional educational water play cannot offer:

- it is moving – physically and mentally;
- it changes dramatically in short periods of time;
- it has direct connection to other living beings;
- it accommodates a larger group spending time together;
- it carries an added value by belonging to a certain landscape or community.

Given that at the heart of natural water play is its quality of being part of a larger scale environment, it is one of the best ways to learn to love and respect the natural world. While playing in it with people who love and understand it, children and young people thrive in the flexible sensory environment where they experience the interconnected cycles of light and dark, seasons, life-cycles, and weather that a river or a lake offers, with no need for additional resources or complicated planning. The natural water environment, adding to the original motivation value of the water as play resource, encourages children to retain their connection to nature into their adult life, based on the positive experience and long-lasting sense of success.

The role of individual learning methods: nature imitating study styles

Individual learning styles have been approached in many different ways by researchers and educators throughout centuries, however a majority agrees that:

- People differ greatly from each other in their preferred ways of processing information.
- The individual differences can be clearly distinguished; each style exhibits very recognisable traits, but cannot be obviously and exclusively named or defined.
- Matching or mismatching learning styles with teaching methods can influence learning significantly (Bedford, 2004).

The different theories of learning highlight different aspects of learning ability: the cognitive process of receiving information, personality, and interaction style.

David Kolb's learning style inventory (1984) works on two levels: a four-stage cycle of learning and four separate learning styles. Kolb's theory is mainly concerned with the learner's *internal cognitive processes*. Effective learning is seen when a person progresses through a cycle of four stages: of having a concrete experience followed by observation of and reflection on that experience, which leads to the formation of abstract concepts (analysis) and generalisations (conclusions), which are then used to test hypotheses in future situations, resulting in new experiences. The learning style inventory includes: diverging (feeling and watching) – people with the ability to look at things from different perspectives; assimilating (watching and thinking) – people who prefer a concise, logical approach; converging (doing and thinking) – people who aim to find solutions to practical issues; and accommodating (doing and feeling) – people who have the ability to learn from primarily 'hands-on' experience, carrying out plans, and involving themselves in new and challenging experiences.

The Myers–Briggs Type Indicator (Myers and McCaulley, 1985) measures personal preferences on four scales derived from Jung's theory of psychological types. People are classified according to their preference for introversion (interest flowing mainly to the inner world of concepts and ideas), extroversion (interest flowing mainly to the outer world of actions, objects, and persons), sensing (tending to perceive immediate, real, practical facts of experience and life), intuition (tending to perceive possibilities, relationships, and meanings of experiences), thinking (tending to make judgements or decisions objectively and impersonally), feeling (tending to make judgements subjectively and personally), judging (tending to act in a planned and decisive way), and perceiving (tending to act in a spontaneous and flexible way).

David Keirsey identifies personal temperament types (Keirsey, 1998) as the artisans (born for action, particularly for artful action), the guardians (who undertake tasks and actions cautiously, and always with careful preparation), the idealists (with an instinct for interpersonal integration) and the rationals (who tend to be organising and planning, or inventing and configuring operations).

H. Gardner's (1985) well-known model of learning styles focuses on the personally preferred way of receiving information, resulting in three types: visual learners (who need to see the teacher's body language and facial expression to fully understand the content of a lesson), auditory learners (who learn best through verbal lectures, listening to tone of voice, pitch) and tactile/kinaesthetic learners (who prefer a hands-on approach, actively exploring the physical world around them).

The Grasha–Riechmann model focuses on student social attitudes toward learning environment, and identifies six types (Riechmann and Grasha, 1974): the avoidant students (having high absenteeism, organising work poorly, taking little responsibility); the responsible participative students (willing to accept responsibility for self-learning, relate well to their peers); the competitive students (suspicious of their peers); the collaborative students (working in harmony with their peers); the dependent students (typically become frustrated when facing new challenges); and the independent students (prefer to work alone).

In Water School, given its unique learning environment, children's learning processes and methods cannot be viewed in the usual educational ways. Influenced by their natural learning style children will learn and make sense by imitation. The cognitive development (or meaning-making) process of the brain happens naturally through experience. Young children's main experience is interaction with the important things (people and other living things, the environment) in their life. This kind of social learning is based on imitating the processes around them. Imitation provides children with possibilities to understand human processes, to practise and perfect new skills, to develop empathy – the ability to view life from another person's point of view. In the Water School environment children are offered a wider range of processes and interactions to imitate, not just those of humans, but those occurring in nature. Imitation presents meaningful lessons to children and leaves lifelong impressions on the developing mind. Children will store images in their mind, and positive and negative experiences can be tested by the brain in the future.

In classic social learning theory Albert Bandura (1977) states that behaviour is learnt from the environment through the process of observational learning. Individuals that are observed are called models. In society children are surrounded by many influential models, such as parents within the family, characters in the media, friends within their peer group, and other adults. These models provide examples of behaviour to observe and imitate. Children pay attention to some of these people (models) and encode their behaviour. At a later time they may imitate or copy the behaviour they have observed.

Similarly to Bandura's social learning model, Water School has special ways of learning based on imitation; however, the Nature Relation Styles are based on more complex processes and occur during children's experience within The Process of Nature Encounter. These learning styles describe children's:

- way of looking at the Water School environment with its natural features and the people within (sensing);
- understanding of the relational processes while being in Water School, including the relationships naturally occurring in the environment; their own relationships with nature, themselves, and others; and other people's relationships to the environment and others (accepting and appreciating);
- methods of immediate processing of information (received from the Water School environment) and the development of thinking through the expression of what has been learnt (understanding);
- creation of the sense of self, separating oneself from the world as a response to the environment (reacting).

During the Water School learning process children encounter nature, experience their own and others' relationship with nature, understand the experience-based information, and use the information to build on their experience. The experience allows and encourages children to multi-task and to actively engage in simultaneous, related, and non-related acts. The provision of open-ended and, simultaneously, rapidly changing resources allows children to see, experience, and gain new knowledge that they can use and shape individually.

The people observer

These children learn best by observation. Observational learning occurs as an outcome of observing, retaining, and replicating behaviour engaged in by others. This observation works as reinforcement, influencing social behaviour, particularly in which responses the children will partake, and it influences the actual acquisition of the response or the response itself significantly less. These children learn from authority figures, both adults and peers. People-observing children in Water School mainly learn by exposure, learning about their environment with a close proximity to other individuals who have different experiences.

   These children:

• spend a long time with others and will choose activities for the company rather than for the activity itself;
• will be showing and sharing each of their discoveries to and with others, and will lead and take part in activities in order to share the experience with others;
• will show interest in the environment from other people's points of view;
• appreciate the Water School environment for its ability to accommodate the group;
• will like group activities, games, discussion.

The environment listener

While environment listener children are observers – as are people observer children – they learn by watching, seeing, and taking part in experiences in a particular environment, rather than by imitation of others. Children, who imitate will likely show a change in behaviour due to observing a person or a group while the environment listeners change due to their own experiences. For the environment listener children the experience within the Water School environment is what acts as a stimulus; they become interested in a particular subject (object, landscape, material etc.) and from watching others interact with the subject. In their case, the interest may or may not lead to increased interest in an object, but may result in direct experience with their subject, which then can result in changed subject-related behaviour.

   These children:

• spend a long time observing and connecting with nature, alone and in like-minded groups;
• will be found in different places, being fascinated by the environment and its features;
• will show interest in the environment by asking questions about it, and by observing materials;
• will appreciate the Water School environment for its environmental beauty and natural offerings;
• will like quiet activities, looking at self-made books, images, gathered objects.

The activator

The activator children learn by active participation. This type of participation does not just mean taking part and being there, but includes the opportunity for the children to express and challenge their inner thoughts and influence decisions while learning new skills, having fun, or developing closer connections with the environment, peers, and adults. Activator children will often change simple ideas of their own or others to reality, activating a learning or play situation, increasing the rate of events happening and ideas flowing.

These children:

- spend time with different activities, led by themselves or others;
- will be found at places where 'actions happen' and will happily follow in order to be able to actively participate, to 'do';
- will show interest in many different subjects by doing and completing;
- will appreciate the Water School environment for its exciting resources and places and for its constantly changing nature;
- will like active times tailored to the place.

The repeater

Repeater children often repeat actions. Doing and hearing something many times helps them to remember information for gradually increasing periods of time. Certain young children particularly need repetition to learn and remember new information; their skills will improve each time an action is repeated. Once children have learnt something, repetition helps them to anticipate what comes next and this accomplishment means that they can participate more actively. Other children also repeat actions for the joy of mastering and to enjoy a new skill. Repetition is a child's way of reminding themselves of what they can do and their method of enjoying the excitement of completion all over again. While learning, the repeater children will personify their experiences – for example animals or others – by repeating experiences (sounds, actions, feelings etc.). They also learn about meaningfulness by repeating. Repeater children, even though appearing to carry out the same action over and over again, carry out a variety of themes rather than doing exactly the same. Children perform repetition to add bits of knowledge, to see how an action changes in varied conditions and what the limits are within their knowledge.

These children:

- spend a long time on one activity;
- will be found at the same place, being occupied with the same activity for a whole session or many sessions;
- will show constant, long-standing interest in a certain subject by asking questions and gathering related material;
- will appreciate the Water School environment for its slow, quiet, and forgiving nature that allows 'mistakes' without consequences;
- will like any activity if given enough time to practise.

The inventor and innovator

Innovator children will plan a process and concentrate on an outcome – activity or product – as their invention. Their ability to invent requires their creativity and imagination; however their creative thinking process often remains covered by the end result. Creative thinking can be applied to children's overall problem-solving, which is what their inventing is all about. Memorising information and the ability to use this information, and knowing what to do with the facts are what inventor children are good at. The process of inventing is extremely highly stimulated by the abundance of engaging materials provided within the Water School environment. Inventor/innovator children differ in their obvious thinking process, which is analytical (the ability to mentally break down an idea or problem into parts and organise it, expressing or involving an analysis of merits and faults), free-flowing (the ability to brainstorm ideas, to express oneself easily and articulately), and open-ended (the ability to see many possibilities, or view objects or situations in different ways, readily being able to change and adapt to different circumstances).

These children:

- perform activities either alone or within a group;
- will be found at different places that appear to be connected and part of a plan;
- will show interest in self-directed subjects and show less interest in other people's ideas;
- will appreciate the Water School environment for its uniqueness, open-ended materials, and endless possibilities;
- will like new places and resources where discovery is always possible.

The experimenter

Just like innovators, experimenter children are little scientists; however, unlike innovators, who work out a process, experimenters will estimate what will happen and are then eager to figure out how everything works, rather than creating something or concentrating on the end result. They do this through 'experiments'. They might throw a pebble and see that it bounces and then throw a shell to see what it will do. They also learn to use objects as tools, for example using an empty oyster shell to try to fill a bucket with water. Their growing memory takes on an important role in helping them learn. They will begin using their new skills, strength, and coordination to conduct 'experiments' on the new ideas and concepts they are learning. When doing experiments, all the areas of children's development are connected to explore and learn. The children's new skills help increase their understanding of how things work by 'testing out' the new ideas and concepts they are learning as experiments to see: 'What will happen if I do this?'

These children:

- spend time with many different activities;
- will be found at different places, with different groups of children;
- will show interest in many different subjects and will be found to use their knowledge in different situations;

- will appreciate the Water School environment for its active nature, for the fact that things happen there on an ongoing basis;
- will like to be stimulated by open-ended questions.

Learning styles refer to children's natural preferences, their habitual and preferred way of receiving, understanding, and memorising new information and skills. In Water School the learning styles are extremely complex and advanced; they are not just individual and consistent but still relational and changing. This means that these learning styles appear as consistent patterns of behaviour but are likely to appear in relation to certain factors. When particular, required factors (meaning human and physical parts of the Water School setting) within the environment are present, the learning style comes into effect.

The practical pedagogy: methodology of teaching in Water School

The methods of teaching within a unique environment need to be in accordance with the environment itself. Effective Water School teaching requires adults' awareness that the importance of variables can influence learning (variables meaning changing factors that occur during the session):

- the learning environment;
- actual experiences in the actual environment (given that one of the unique characteristics of Water School is its ever-changing nature, the actual experience of a Water School session will be different every time the site is entered as the site itself is different every time);
- the learner's individual learning behaviour;
- the learning group, including the teacher.

The teaching methodology classically means the principles and methods used for instructing children in a learning environment. Commonly used teaching methods can be instructor-directed, research-based, or collaboration-centred. Within the instructor-directed approach the instructor is the main authority figure and the children passively receive information via lectures and instruction with assessment at the end. Research-based learning appreciates children's ability to conduct hands-on investigation, which the teacher facilitates by providing the theme, the resources, and guidance. Collaboration-centred teaching allows and organises group-work and encourages individual learners to take responsibility for their own learning. The classic teaching methods include many different elements: demonstration, explanation, memorisation, participation, organisation, learning by teaching peers, or a combinations of these. In the classic classroom environment the choice of teaching method or methods depends on:

- the information the teacher aims to give;
- the skill the teachers aim to teach;
- the individual children and their relationship to learning;
- group dynamics.

Water School education is based on the classic elements of teaching; however it is more complex than the classroom. This programme has the children and their learning process at the centre with a complex, skilled – but invisible – support role of the educator; however the outcome is not necessarily defined other than having personal growth as an objective of teaching and the environment taking a major and unique role. The environment's unpredictable and rapidly changing nature affects the variables of teaching: the learning environment, the learning experience, and the behaviour of the individuals and the group. In a Forest School – although noticing and studying the change of environment – the programme is based on a similarly set programme during each session and based on children's personal learning, but in a Water School one of the major aims is the acceptance of change and studying the effect of the rapid environmental change on the individual learning process. Given that the change often happens in the course of a Water School session (e.g. tides coming in quickly, rain affecting the level of river water, edge of pond changes due to a local flood etc.), this programme offers the children a larger variety of environmental opportunities, where the regular feature and routine is guaranteed by their innate connection to water.

The Child-Led, Occurrence-Driven Operation Process (COOP)

The COOP describes a framework in which children's environment-based and change-accommodating learning process takes place, while expressing the stages of the children's growth process influenced by the environmental experience. This is not a linear process but a constant cycle, with defined but interlinked and moving elements (see Figure 3.1). It is led by the children's personal characteristics and interest and it is driven by the occurrence of the actual experiences in the actual (Water School) environment. The 'operation' does not necessarily mean that the children are doing something or are occupied with an activity in the classic sense of 'being busy', but rather refers to the action of functioning or the fact of being active or in effect within the environment. The children can experience the process partially or complete the cycle; they can go through it once or repeatedly during each single Water School session.

Sensing and memorising is the phase of provocation, where the environment – and the children's first experience within it – inspires them as an individual or as part of a group to make some actions or express some feelings. Provocation also means to induce activity of any kind with an underlying sense of awakening from inactivity, to stir sudden – sometimes strong – feelings but maybe not characteristic actions. As children encounter the 'big world', its naturally inviting impulses act as provocation – a catalyst for the children's development process, stimulating millions of neurons.

When children encounter the external environment around them for the first time, they use all their senses to gather information in order to make personal sense of their experience. Their developing brain stores the information and accesses it when similar things are encountered again. This strengthens connections in the brain, and as regular Water School sessions ensure there are opportunities for such encounters and for similar experiences to be re-lived, the experiences become memories that they can recall during each Water School visit, until the experience/skill/impression becomes embedded, enabling new experiences to be built upon them. Through the experience,

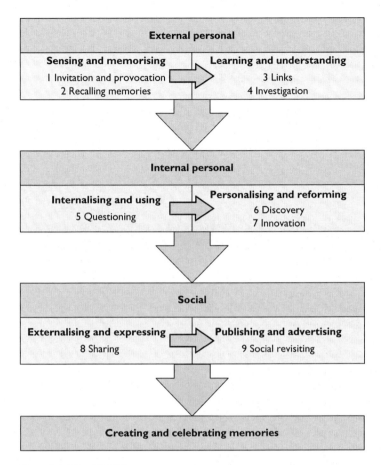

Figure 3.1 The COOP process

and the experience-stimulated action, a fact, skill, or other knowledge will bring up a memory or thought in the child's mind for processing. This is an important factor of the Water School learning process; the actual experience in a Water School session can be significantly different from that in a previous session and memories create the building blocks of learning. This does not necessarily mean that the children would need to possess previous knowledge in a particular subject related to Water School; it could mean a simple skill – for example, in order to reach a wanted pebble a baby remembers how to move forward.

Learning and understanding: once memories have been stored, the developing brain accesses the information enabling the child to make and recognise connections or links between things, feelings etc. When the child is comfortable with their environment based on the familiarity achieved by the connections in the brain, the child will start to investigate further and examine their own reactions. The Water School environment is an ideal setting for learning as it provides the right balance of familiar and new experiences (for example, trees are always standing in the same place, the bridge is static, while the riverbank can change and animals keep appearing and disappearing). Therefore in this phase children create means of contact (links), to enable communication between their own experiences, between themselves and the process, and between themselves and others, where one affects the other. In this phase the children create a chain of interconnected skills and knowledge to assist understanding, which creates the opportunity for further learning. In the light of new experiences the recalled previous knowledge might alter or gain new meaning in the Water School, which will often motivate the children to search for facts through a detailed or careful examination.

Internalising and using: after gathering ample information about their experiences, children will develop new brain connections, directed by their own, internal personal thoughts and methods; they become motivated to question how things work, why things happen in a certain way, what they could do to preserve or change things, how they could use their existing knowledge to probe and challenge things, and how they feel about what they encounter. In this process they will discover new connections, and they will use the information in their own unique way to innovate, to make a difference, and to add a personal touch. In nature, there is a vast array of impulses that provide information for children. The questioning phase refers to the expression of the inquiry that invites the children to further develop their investigation skills or calls for a reply. It also means highlighting a point, which opens their mind to controversy and to consideration. In this sense, the questioning is a method of investigation and analysis.

Personalising and reforming: children have a variety of ways in which they store, remember, combine, and express information gathered through their experiences. They make sense of information by using it in their play, mimicking the world (people and events) around them. Via their play they refresh and reform the way things can be used, the way their inner thoughts can be expressed, and the way others can be approached. Regular attendance at Water School sessions provides children with familiarity and a safe base from which they can explore and develop, as well as providing stimuli to generate effective learning. The discovery phase covers a vast variety of activities that the children do in order to notice or learn, especially by making an effort. On the group learning level it covers being the first, or the first of one's group, to find, learn about, or observe something, while personally it means to learn about something for the first time in one's experience. In the Water School environment it also means the appreciation of others – to identify another person as a potential source to learn from or be fascinated by.

Just like the discovery phase, the innovation phase can also happen on a group or personal level. In its group form it can mean the introduction of something new for the group or a summary of the results of a group-learning situation. On an individual level it can mean the creation of something in the mind or the act of starting something for the first time. Children can invent many different things: a skill, a theory, or scheme to fit a purpose, or they can invent an object or any creation as the result of their questioning, negotiation, and discovery process.

Expressing and externalising: children express and externalise their inner thought processes for a variety of reasons, starting from the moment they are born, given that humans have an innate need to socialise and share experiences. They use a variety of ways to express their thoughts in their play, which is a deep and complex communication method. They externalise their thoughts naturally to gain the opinion of another person (an outsider from their inner world), and to probe and test their view. Sharing in the Water School context means to allow someone to use and experience jointly, and enjoy something. This sharing is an interdependent relationship between the different entities: the children share to show, to be proud, to challenge, and to reflect. It is an act of giving but in the sense of requesting review or reaction, even if the reaction is simply shared joy.

Publishing and advertising: once children have reached their own conclusions (this process can vary in time from a minute to several weeks), they are able to use their knowledge to make social connections in various ways, which will maintain the progress of their learning journey. They externalise their inner thoughts to socialise, but they will publish and advertise them to establish their own place in the community, and to learn to defend their position, while learning vital social skills (communicating, negotiating, challenging, accepting, sharing etc.) in the process. The revisiting phase covers both the physical and mental meaning of viewing again.

Revisiting is a tool for connecting prior experience to further learning, where the act of revisiting is to recall past experiences as a starting point for further exploration of new ideas (Rinaldi, 1998). This happens immediately in the context of the learning experience, a natural alternative to the instant video reviewing of the classroom environment introduced by Forman (1999), which displays events on the viewing screen right after they happen. While Forman simply suggested instant reviewing for the understanding of differences between appropriate and inappropriate social reactions, in the Water School environment the social revisiting gains a more complex meaning: it covers reflection on and a summary of the children's learning process, including sharing, reviewing, valuing, evaluating, and challenging the outcome of the process.

Creating and celebrating memories: gaining approval from significant others is important to children. The celebration of the learning process and any kind of achievement is often used to increase children's motivation. The celebration is a social focus on the children's efforts and achievements, specifically acknowledging the processes of completing an activity or solving a problem. It does not just mean a festive display. Celebration in the COOP means scaffolding – the process, just as used on a building site, means supporting. It also means appreciation and awe. It means sharing and advertising in a way that makes the children themselves the experts. When children are ready to share information, thoughts and feelings, they become equally ready to accept those of others, and they will ultimately be able to understand and appreciate their own uniqueness as part of their immediate community, so they can start new experiments, taking on more and more learning by building from their memories.

This type of learning, as described in the COOP cycle, can actually occur in a preset situation as well (for example indoors in a classroom); however in the Water School environment it is a natural process, natural learning. Natural learning means believing in children's natural affinity toward acquiring new skills and finding out new information, regardless of the method of teaching, so learning should take place in a natural manner without any connection to the usual institution of school and curriculum. Natural learning is a very ancient – although still viewed as post-modern – form of education, separated from the usual offering of a school. It does not mean that adults do not have a role; instead of them imposing their ideas of the learning required on children, they offer aspirations and choose to allow their children to develop their own priorities for learning and to find their own learning methods and direction. During these processes adults also support children by providing a rich and stimulating environment in which to learn, an environment that always has resources available for learning, assisting, and providing feedback and encouragement when required to do so and in a form the children need and accept. This type of truly natural learning occurs as a result of the children's self-directed development and own motivations, through which they become confident and independent learners. When the natural learning taking place in the Water School environment, some of the resources are spontaneously guaranteed. Effective natural learning requires key factors, the *STEPS*:

1   Space

Children benefit greatly from having physical space that is theirs to play in. Children – especially a group of children – need spaces that meet the needs of different ages and stages at the same time, where children's different play structures are allowed by use of the space. Playability means the physical, historical, and biological characteristics and resource offering of a space.

2   Time

Children are nurtured and schooled by their parents to prepare them for a happy, fulfilled life where they will be able to make appropriate choices; on the whole, what counts in their future is how they handle the issues in their lives. Schooling is supposed to educate children, however most issues in life cannot be solved with the type of answers and methods learnt within the usual curriculum. The real problems of life (social and emotional) require the ability to process, think, judge, control, and create. Children learn the basic concepts through early years play as the skills to cooperate, process, empathise, or feel cannot be taught: they are practised in play. Practice needs time.

3   Exploration

Children learn by exploring their environment. Exploring is normal and important for children as it is one of the first steps in learning about objects and in learning how to solve problems. Children are fascinated about how things work, what they look like, and how they are created or made. Skills are learnt more quickly in a challenge-rich environment while exploring and testing their environment.

4   People

Many educational researchers have observed that the majority of children's knowledge is acquired through observation and imitation, learning from role models, and imitating the behaviours of those they admire (Bandura, 1971; Meltzoff, 1988). While parents are the most important role models for children, educators can have an equally positive effect on children's lives by highlighting the importance of intellectual curiosity. Although children are naturally keen observers, in their early years of development they tend seek the safety of adult support, and while the challenge, exploration, and resources are naturally provided by the environment in the Water School programme, adults strongly influence children's personal attitudes and relationships with their experiences.

5   Sustainability

In the Water School programme, sustainability of education means to teach children to meet their basic needs and improve their own well-being without affecting the quality of life for future generations. According to Tilbury and Wortman (2004) sustainability of education is achievable simply by helping the children to acquire basic skills: envisioning (understand the future, imagine and plan how to improve the environment and people's lives within); critical thinking and reflection (gain knowledge, perspective, and opinions and learn how to use it); systemic thinking (acknowledging the complex order of the world and to find solutions to problems); building partnerships (using communication effectively to be able to work together); and participation in decision-making – empowering people.

The specific learning environment and child-led approach of the Water School programme needs specific methods to accommodate children's learning. Observation is a fundamental way for humans to learn about their environment and the other humans within. People are physically and mentally programmed to recognise and memorise detailed information about our environment through our senses, but within the education of Water School observation of children is more than just looking or listening, it is making a connection, understanding, and planning.

Observation is the main and basic method of teaching in Water School; it fundamentally defines and further shapes the adult behaviour within the environment, which than makes this type of education sustainable and tailored for the children, without directly affecting the environment. Environment-specific observation methods ensure that the children can enjoy a free relationship with the environment without adult intervention, but with plenty of adult support to develop their own progress further. These types of observation methods are complex, conditional, and focus on children's relationship with nature – on their actual experience within the actual environment. Some of the observation methods are simultaneous with the experience itself and some of them, occurring afterwards, aim to explore the outcome of the session or its effect on the children.

The field-based observation tool

This observation method is based on the classic method of a running record, in the sense of the adult following the child and recording what happens. They are closely analysing interactions and the progress of a child; however the focus is not on recording the list of events in a detailed way, but observing how the child feels when experiencing the environment and through that experience acquires a particular new skill. The recording happens in preset categories; however the key objective is to fill in the detail factually about what is seen at the time it occurs. The aim of this observation is to better understand the learning that occurs when inspired by the environment.

Practically, this observation happens at the beginning of a session, when the child first starts to interact with the environment. The adult observes the first three things the child interacts with (touches, uses, talks to, watches etc.) and records whether:

1 *the child's behaviour is*: 'observational' (watches, listens from a distance), explorative (tries, touches, smells, lifts, etc.), or investigative (uses, incorporates, manipulates, challenges);
2 *the experience is*: sensory (personal and focuses on feelings), physical (active, 'doing'), or social.

The information recorded on this observation will assist the educators in understanding the child's preferred learning process and the adults' ability to support the child's learning in line with their nature relation style.

The 'me by me' observation method

Photographs of children are important tools of reflection and revisiting, however when reviewed together with the children, they provide even more information about children's learning processes. When making observations, educators can easily avoid being judgemental or biased in their interpretations by involving children in the interpretation and by asking children to provide an accurate picture of what they actually see. Selecting the most appropriate and effective recording technique usually depends on the particular focus and purpose of the record itself, meaning that records may take many forms, however photographs are accurate pictures of a particular moment.

In this observation method the adults take photographs of the children at different times within a session. After the session they present the photos to the children and find an appropriate method to listen to the children's thoughts about the moment, the related feelings, and the learning that has taken place. The expressions can be: verbal, by drawing, or – with younger children – simply pointing. This way educators gain an accurate account about the children's personal thoughts and feelings, together with the knowledge of what the children find important, remarkable, or significant in an experience. This can help the child to understand their own learning, while also assisting the adult in how to support the child most appropriately.

The Water School interaction method

This observation method focuses on children's personal relationships with the environment. Although this relationship is much more than physical, it is instigated, initiated, and further motivated by the physical parts and objects within the Water School environment. The Water School interaction method is a structured observation technique where the educator observes the children's experiences after the actual Water School session, while the observed child recalls and reflects on their own learning experience by interacting with an object or a representation of an object transported from the Water School session.

The child is given a set of five objects (or representations of objects) and (if appropriate for the child's age) asked five questions that are designed to investigate the quality and nature of the child's relationship to the experience. It is identifying areas of strength and of difficulty through the relationship and assists the child in understanding their own thought processes. The questions to ask children are:

- *What would you use this for?*
- *Have you thought about where it comes from?*
- *Have you thought about whose this is?*
- *How can you find out about what this is/where it comes from?*
- *What happens/do you think will happen when you have this?*
- *How do you feel when you have this?*
- *How could you change this?*

The interaction is videoed and then shown to the child, while commented on with positive observations. Very young children still benefit from the experience by seeing themselves and their own reactions.

The numerical scale of Water School behaviour

The purpose of this observation method is to help educators with collecting and sharing information about how young children deal with their learning experience in Water School and what they pay specific attention to, through the use of a systematic and strategic observation. The focus of this method is children's natural ability to cope with changes.

The observation rates children's behaviour on a simple scale in basic situations, where children's engagement, expression, peer interaction, adult interaction, activity, physical attitude, and communication is evaluated and classed as:

1   Not at all characteristic (1 point)
2   Somewhat characteristic (2 points)
3   Just like the child (3 points).

The situation (what is the child doing and where?)	Not at all characteristic	Somewhat characteristic	Just like the child
Engagement			
Expression			
Peer interaction			
Adult interaction			
Activity			
Physical attitude			
Communication			

Points are given and totalled. The maximum is 21, which would mean that the child copes well with the situation and the environment. This is a valuable tool to help recognise and respond to the needs of individual children, providing specific, developmentally appropriate information to assist educators in supporting the children. Educators observe the children engaging in individual, large, and small group activities, participating, interacting, and displaying already learnt behaviour; by paying attention and simply evaluating, educators can reflect on what they observe to gain an understanding of children's skills and abilities. By documenting what is seen, educators can begin to create a profile of individual children's strengths and needs within the Water School environment that aids their future education.

The movement observation tool

This observation focuses on children's movements, which contain important information about children's aptitude and attitude toward their Water School experience. It looks at children's acts of motion based on three categories at different times (minimum three) during a Water School session or at consecutive sessions and evaluates how it changes.

The situation (what is the child doing and where?)		
Physical characteristics of the movement	Large	Small
Emotional characteristics of the movement	Intense	Weak
Speed of movement	Quick/sudden	Slow
Aim of movement	Movement for purpose	Purpose is the movement

Adding evidence and comments will help the educator understand the differences in movement and will support the effective use of the movement observation tool.

The timing and method of observations in Water School depends on the circumstances, on the child, and on the experience of the child; they can be planned and spontaneous. The varied use of these techniques will provide a relatively complete picture of the children; however, it will always be conducted with no claim of being exhaustive or complete.

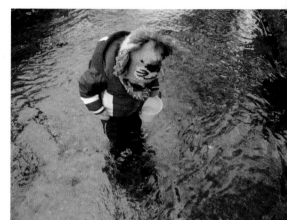

Chapter 4

How children learn holistically in Water School

Introduction

This chapter will set out to answer practitioners' questions and allay their anxieties about delivering the Water School programme by describing the way children learn through natural water and by providing curriculum links and example session plans. The chapter will also briefly discuss how special educational needs can be catered for within the programme and touch upon the presentation of play therapy within this environment. The chapter will provide possible activity ideas to support practitioners setting up their own practice.

Ron Miller, the founder of the journal *Holistic Education Review* explains holistic education as a philosophy of education:

> [. . .] based on the premise that each person finds identity, meaning, and purpose in life through connections to the community, to the natural world, and to spiritual values such as compassion and peace. Holistic education aims to call forth from people an intrinsic reverence for life and a passionate love of learning.
>
> (Miller, n.d.)

The Water School programme delivers holistic education based on the automatically inviting, open-ended, and versatile nature of the environment.

Young children are extremely interested in the earth and nature, and something that is so innate will provide the perfect environment for playing, exploring, engaging, learning actively, and thinking creatively and critically. The natural forms of water and the surrounding environment host the best opportunities for effective education and learning. As this feature is not always accessible for the children of today's society, Water School can quickly become a place of conversations where everyone can do exactly what they want to do at the time.

The resources around natural water (mud, sticks, pebbles, shells, grass) instigate many questions and can evidence many topics and subjects from maths, through creativity, to literacy. It is possible to create good subject knowledge when shared with the children through creative thinking, at the same time pretending and acting out many different social situations. This simplifies planning as it allows children to lead and choose their learning objectives, needing only simple, suitable strategies that are effectively chosen to evidence – rather than deliver – learning in all areas. Letting children lead results in both educators and children having high levels of expectation toward themselves and each other and it challenges their knowledge.

Water School play also encourages high expectations of behaviour and good use of time, where prior learning and assessment is used for informing educators about each individual. The children themselves use their own memories to carry on or not, to enhance, or just conduct variations of activities each time, so these possibilities reinforce and extend learning. Being in charge, children feel valued and are actively involved in the learning process, building on mutual trust and respect. When playing in Water School children are naturally encouraged to achieve; they are given the opportunity to enjoy a genuine sense of achievement where independent work is encouraged and access to resources is easy. Knowledge gained during Water School play is easy to transfer to other disciplines. When creations are made with natural resources and left out in the natural environment – some for everyone to see, some hidden, some exposed to traffic, and some inside nature features – revisiting the creations provides a great deal of information about our world. As an outcome of this effective, natural education children will learn by:

- exploring and discovering
- experimenting and investigating
- getting to know and shaping their own environment
- engaging thoughts, senses and inner self
- imagining, planning and creating
- connecting with nature, solving problems
- communicating, listening, and socialising.

In their early years children are widely interested in the world around them and the water-based outdoor environment provides unique opportunities to educate them within play and tailored to their own individual needs. A Water School programme for the early years can influence and foster many areas of development in young children, including emotional (self-motivation, appreciation, emotional intelligence, being and working with others, taking turns etc.), physical (balance, coordination, strength, perseverance), and cognitive (thinking skills, communication, knowledge of the world). In the Water School programme, children's holistic development progresses, while adults working with the children gain a greater opportunity to learn about them. Throughout the Water School sessions children are allowed to repeat their actions and exhibit their inner world through their innate connection to the water world. Recognisable forms of behaviour will take place in the new environment and gain a new level of meaning for the children and the adults around them. By using careful observation to witness and identify children's learning and to support them in their preferred way of purposeful play, adults can significantly deepen children's learning in a completely natural way.

The water-sensing procedure: AID

Around and within the water-based environment, young children – who still have a strong, innate relation to water – are more able to enter their inner world of self (thoughts, feelings, and processes) that ultimately helps them to understand the world that is outside the self. Children go through a *water-sensing procedure*, during which the water-based environment becomes the method of communication or frame and the carried information or means. Similarly to multisensory integration, children gather information from different sensory modalities – such as sight, sound, touch, smell, self-motion, and taste – and the information is integrated by the nervous system. Through the water the information processing ability develops, and children show extremely high levels of interest, relaxation, and exploration. Their memory output grows considerably and their complex combining ability develops.

The water-sensing procedure (AID) consists of three basic processes:

1   *Absorbing and internalising*: the children react to the water environment and via the changes in their body they observe their own reactions to the water;
2   *Integrating and colliding*: in the second phase, after familiarising themselves with their own emotional and physical reactions, children become able to merge their bodies with the water, while realising that there is a 'vice versa' effect, and as a reaction children begin to externalise some of their feelings;
3   *Deconstructing and reconstructing (forming)*: using the water to deconstruct their inner processes (emotional and physical reactions to the water) the children reconstruct their own conscious thought and unconscious feelings to create responses to the world around them.

During the water-sensing procedure children's play becomes really intense, complex, and deep, creating a dialogue between the inner and the outer world via the connection of water. Children have different ways of going through this procedure, depending on their thinking skills and level of understanding. Some children spend more time in each phase from session to session, while others go through the process repeatedly within one session. When considering the activities offered in sessions, using AID can help practitioners to provide a greater and broader variety of learning experiences.

Delivering Water School sessions can be a very exciting prospect for children and adults alike, however to fully embrace the philosophy of the programme, adults need to apply a very flexible and open teaching approach. People's perceptions of the water world can differ greatly and the general disposition, nature, and nurture of a person can affect and alter the outcome of the Water School programme significantly. Gradual introduction to the experience helps the children and adults to learn about the water world through observation, noticing, exploring, and naming. Water School programmes may have different outcomes, but all Water School education is successful in the sense of having an effect on the adults and children and providing the entrance to an area of magic that stimulates curiosity and imagination, regardless of whatever the effect, change, or stimulation is.

Session overview

Young children need continuous repetition to help them remember information and build their memory. The application of the Pareto principle (also known as the 80–20 rule or the law of the 'vital few') helps to understand the role repetition plays in the learning process. In young children's learning the Pareto rule means that in learning cycles 80 per cent of information should be familiar to the children, so they can comfortably remember the new, 20 per cent of the session information. The Pareto principle can also be applied to the education itself. The educators need to focus their teaching goals on just a few important learning needs, being the 'vital few' areas. By concentrating on only the vital few needs, the achievements within these areas are likely to be much greater, therefore other learning areas can be positively affected by the sense of success and self-growth.

After having experienced situations or explored resources many times, a child will probably be able to memorise basic methods and characteristics well enough to form an individual understanding or create a personalised meaning. Children need to feel successful. In order to learn how to do something well, children need to practise again and again, until an understanding is gained and success is achieved. Once children have mastered skills they will be able to repeat actions for pure enjoyment and they will also be equipped to try their knowledge in new contexts and link existing and new knowledge and information. Repetition is also a child's way to build confidence and trust, a sense of trust in their own abilities. Repetition helps children to anticipate what they are looking forward to, which ultimately helps them to accept change and learn from differences, making sense of the world in the process.

The uniqueness and exceptional educational value of the Water School environment lies in its characteristic of providing certainty and change at the same time. During a Water School programme children will visit the same environment repeatedly, where the environment is the same on a large scale; its features, however, are constantly changing within single sessions, as well as from session to session.

Session 1: meet the environment, find landmarks around the water, set boundaries, discuss safety of self and environment, and learn basic methods to assess immediate risks;

Session 2: create a sense of belonging by developing a basic understanding of the environment, review landmarks and observe their changes, express preferences, look at the environment's natural resources;

Session 3: explore the water world habitat and its occupants; discuss the effects of human activity on the environment by studying ways to protect it;

Session 4: explore the self as part of the water habitat; discuss the effects of the environment on human feelings, well-being, and activity;

Session 5: find ways to harmonise the self with the environment; use knowledge to protect the environment and its occupants;

Session 6: apply knowledge and skills to develop the self within the environment and thrive in positive relationships with the self, others, and the environment.

The sessions can be delivered using a large variety of activities; however, the main focus needs to remain on the overall personality growth of the children, achieved by working through the activities and tackling the areas of development. The uniqueness of Water School originates from children's special relationship with the water environment and from the process of self-development based on children being in their element. Given the focus on the water environment, the main educational objective is hosting the relationship between the children and the environment and continuously developing the naturally occurring opportunities for this relationship to evolve. The sessions are not structured in the usual meaning of lesson structure; rather they are built around children's personal relationship with the environment. The process of relationship forming is what determines the framework of the Water School sessions:

1   meeting/greeting the environment;
2   choosing an occupation, based on personal state of mind (interest, attitude, knowledge, memories);
3   entering the environment and forming an active relationship (at this point children usually decide to join a group or engage individually);
4   personal achievement (feeling, success, discovery, exploration);
5   sharing and expression of achievement, closely connected to and contained by the environment;
6   recalling memories.

Each session may be built on a similar framework, so young children can find security in repetition and stability, which ultimately helps them to explore their environment – and themselves within – further, and step out of their comfort zone, even if only for a short while. The group of children usually has a set routine of introduction and welcoming, and while it is traditionally a circle-time type of activity, in Water School the strong focus on the environment inspires the exploring of different types of introduction, for example:

•   Children are encouraged to take a short walk, pick up an object (stone, stick, sand, leaf etc.), sit down, and feel the object.
•   One child is asked to walk to the water feature in the local environment, return to the group, and describe it (very young children are transported to the water and the others observe).
•   Children are encouraged to quietly engage with the environment in their individual secret place.

Children are encouraged to assess risks for themselves during these initial activities, with simple, motivating instructions given in the form of observations, questions, and wonderings (e.g. 'I have seen a . . . have you seen it?' or 'I am wondering whether you will find a . . . '), that are 'things to notice' rather than things to do.

Water School programmes can have themes such as old fisherman, wildlife homes, or a particular animal/plant around the water that children wish to explore. The themes can help young children to motivate their own interest and create links between sessions. For young babies the focus is sensory exploration within the environment, to create and maintain a confident and interested way of thinking within the environment. Practitioners need to aim at finding the links and understanding each individual child's relationship with the water environment, so that they can support children without leading them. Activities are then offered for children to choose freely and information is given about small achievable tasks, ensuring full inclusiveness where the children help one another in group cohesion. Water School has a strong personal–social–environmental ethos. Free play is the main element of all sessions, enabling practitioners to complete specific observations, in order to use the information to motivate children's valuable discoveries. Group gathering activity closes the sessions where the practitioner will probe children's memories by repeating events from the session or through revisiting objects used by the children in the session. This has the complex objective of sharing, memorising, and deepening accelerated learning, while also reminding the children how they feel or what they have achieved. Through this method children's confidence, trust (in their own abilities and those of others), and skills rapidly build.

The Water School programme with its focus on water provides a well-rounded learning, as the children gain information in sensory and extra-sensory ways. These include all data received – not just information accumulated through the recognised physical senses, but the way it is sensed, processed, and utilised by the mind. This complex learning is stimulated by the presence of the innate human reaction to water and its rapidly changing characteristics and different physical states. For example, when a child sees, touches, or otherwise explores natural water, he or she builds on the physical level of the experience and an immediate thinking process is triggered: 'Where does the water go?' 'How does water go under the ground?' 'Why do the stones and my toes look different under water?' 'What does water feel like?'

The way babies learn in Water School

Babies are sensory motor learners. When newly born, babies have a well-developed sense of touch overall, but a less sharp finger pad sensitivity and – due to nature's programmed survival instinct – the majority of their senses are concentrated around certain areas on their bodies, for example their lips. To aid babies' development, adults need to ensure there is a sensory-rich environment with many textures, temperatures, colours, smells, and sounds where the babies feel comfortable and interested to explore. Given that babies' innate relation to water is even closer than that of the toddler or young children, the Water School environment is perfectly suitable for babies as all their senses are stimulated by the availability of rich sensory experiences. Their physical development is advancing to new levels in response to the many different sources of stimuli; the varied environmental stimulates the babies to become motivated to move their bodies in many different ways; they are encouraged to learn. Being around natural water also supports babies' physical confidence, as their movements are more natural in water; this ultimately motivates children to concentrate on other activities, rather than on movement itself. The special environment has a great impact on babies' development of vision, hearing, and touch too. Their brains – in response to the demands of coping with the vast array of new information – motivated by the stimuli, build new neural pathways that contribute to the early learning process. The increased activity of the brain helps to advance all areas of development; while receiving and learning to decode new information, the developing brain also has to store, use, and link the information at the same time. Motivated by senses, the brain feeds back to its 'informers' – the sensors of the body – and while demanding more information the brain concentrates its activity not only on survival, but learning. The abilities of the young mind become wider and deeper, and the interactions between the brain cells prepare the young child for the all-important communication stage, which will be the main learning method in subsequent years. In order to take advantage of the body's ability to improve through sensory motor learning, the brain must be given ample opportunity to recognise and understand productive and counterproductive information, based on basic movements of the body during activity. Neurophysiologists observed that conventional exercises – with their focus on muscular effort, force, and speed – inhibit the brain's ability to function properly on the body's behalf and it becomes impossible for the brain to make the clear sensory distinctions needed to improve the body's organisation (Lees and Hopkins,

2013). When, however, movements are slow and effortless they will activate the brain's movement centres and generate a flow of valuable information between the brain cells. In Water School, where time and space are given to allow slow and concentrated movements, the brain is allowed to be free to make important sensory distinctions.

Curriculum learning: links and activities

The typical educational areas of child development differ in different countries.

A classic summary of the learning areas (Piaget and Inhelder, 1969) groups the skills and abilities into five areas of human development:

1   Physical development: the changes in size, shape, and physical maturity of the body, including physical abilities and coordination.
2   Intellectual development: the learning and use of language; the ability to reason, problem-solve, and organise ideas; it is related to the physical growth of the brain.
3   Social development: the process of gaining the knowledge and skills needed to interact successfully with others.
4   Emotional development: feelings and emotional responses to events; changes in understanding one's own feelings and appropriate forms of expressing them.
5   Moral development: the growing understanding of right and wrong, and the change in behaviour caused by that understanding; sometimes called a conscience.

Alaska's Early Childhood Investment (Best Beginnings, n.d.) mentions five other areas:

1   Physical health, well-being, and movement skills: these activities are designed to help develop children's large and small muscle control, their coordination, and physical fitness.
2   Social and emotional development: activities in this area target children's ability to make and keep social relationships, with adults and with other children, while learning to recognise and express their own feelings more effectively. They gain experience understanding and responding to the emotions of others.
3   Approaches to learning: children differ in how they approach new tasks, difficult problems, or challenges. These activities spark children's curiosity, interest, and attention, and the ability to stay on task.
4   Thinking abilities and general knowledge: the suggestions in this area help children to figure out how the world works and how things are organised, 'learning how to learn', improving problem-solving ability, and abstract thinking.
5   Communication, language, and literacy: these activities help children in learning to express themselves and to understand what others say.

The British national curriculum Early Years Foundation Stage separates three prime and four specific areas (Department for Education, 2014):

1   personal, social and emotional development: making relationships, self-confidence, self-awareness, managing feelings and behaviour;
2   physical development: moving and handling, health and self-care;
3   communication and language: listening and attention, understanding and speaking;

4   literacy: reading and writing;
5   mathematics: numbers, shape, space, and measure;
6   understanding the world: people and communities, the world;
7   expressive arts and design: exploring and using media and materials, being imaginative.

On their journey to adulthood children first need to develop their confidence by trusting familiar places where they spend time with others to achieve a state of emotional safety and well-being, only then they will be ready to receive information. Children's emotional confidence grows simultaneously with gaining physical well-being, allowing them to physically follow their interests and explore. The confident child is ready to make valuable connections through the means of communication and it inspires the child to leave their individual stamp (physical and mental) on their environment (the physical environment and other people). As the children grow and have more and more experiences they become able to express their thoughts and use their own ideas to affect their own learning in a creative way. Along this journey children will develop an understanding of concepts in the world, and make sense of their own lives.

The exact manner of this maturing process is unique to each child and necessarily needs to occur of its own accord, following its own path, so it cannot be achieved or even hurried through preset activities that are planned or directed by adults. However, a sound understanding of how it can be encouraged and advanced via activity suggestions and ideas from the educators can move along the learning progress significantly. Therefore, the educators of Water School are advised to think of possibilities in their own environment that help (rather than direct) the children in a relaxed way and also ensure the children gain the most from the experience. As children learn by copying, suggestion and modelling are often necessary to spark the children.

The areas of learning in Water School include all the skills, knowledge, and experiences that young infants and children need to grow, learn, and develop, and reach their full potential. The areas of learning are:

- confidence and emotional well-being;
- physical well-being;
- communication and social connections;
- marks;
- expression and creativity;
- understanding and creation of concepts, logical and mathematical meaning-making.

Confidence and emotional well-being

The early years of development play a vital role in determining mental health throughout one's life. The objectives of confidence-building and the development of emotional well-being are to nurture mentally healthy children, giving them knowledge of their personal identity and a sense of self. Children in a state of emotional well-being have the ability to recognise and manage emotions, to form relationships, and to deal with difficult situations. Children's emotional well-being is the result of healthy development within a nurturing environment, with secure emotional attachments that will form the foundation for future mental health and have far-reaching effects on developing emotional and social skills, thus enabling their future health and attainment. In the Water School environment children automatically gain a different perspective. They view themselves in a spacious environment and, through their innate relationship with water, their deep level of thinking and relaxation is triggered. Activities in this area show the children how they can connect to the environment, what mark they can leave on the environment, and how they can treasure their memories related to the Water School environment.

Understanding of the physical self and body awareness

Knowledge of the physical self and body awareness is the understanding of one's own body: its shape, its size, and where and how it is moving. It is important as it involves combining and making sense of information from the sensory systems of balance, touch, and positioning; the more effectively one can do this, the better one's physical awareness will be.

Children achieve awareness of the physical self throughout their daily activities; however, their understanding can be aided by organised opportunities to learn about their own bodies.

PLASTER OF PARIS HAND AND FOOTPRINTS

Mix water with the sand/earth/other ground surface to enable the creation of a deep mould. Place children's hands/feet deep into the sand and ask them to push down hard. (For small children push down each little finger and toe deeper into the sand.) Mix up the plaster of Paris with the children as directed (usually 1 part plaster to 2 parts water) in a sand bucket with some water (from the river, lake, or sea), then gently pour the plaster mixture into the moulds, using a small stick to help guide the plaster mix throughout the mould if necessary. Drying takes at least 30 minutes, so it is best to do this activity soon after arriving.

FOOTPRINTS

At the end of each session children can go on a footprint hunt. During this activity they can be asked to find/identify their own footprints, and/or compare them to those of others. They are asked supporting questions and are given pointers to observe how big the area is they played in and what other people/creatures visited the area; this helps them to review their own learning. They can be asked to make a map of footprints they found (smaller children are assisted to learn that their feet leave a print). This helps the children to understand more about themselves and others; it helps them to view their own mark on the environment.

MUD OR SAND BATH

When children seem a little wary of entering the water, nurturing activities can be introduced, such as bathing and pampering. These help regulate and calm the children, enhance their self-worth, and provide worthwhile experiences of empathetic responses to their need for comfort, safety, and reassurance. When children use mud or wet sand on the skin during a playful mud bath, building on the relaxing quality of the mud or sand they can learn to accept and provide secure soothing when needing comfort. They can check each other for pains and bruises, and provide a comforting, safe touch: a bit of 'magic' motivated by their love of others. Developing further on touch as an essential part of physical development – giving muddy foot treatment by covering each other's feet with mud, watching them dry and crack, making muddy footprints – will help children to find their own place in a group and develop a sense of community.

THE WATER MIRROR

By using the water surface as a mirror, the burden and over-excitement of meeting one's self-image can become fun and different. This activity can be carried out in many different ways: children can observe their own image as it reflects in the water; children can dress up and change their look differently to their peers. Through this activity children can process the psychological transference they often experience within their daily lives. The transference is the unconscious redirection of feelings from one person to another, or often the repetition in the present of something that was important (feelings about a life event, emotions in a relationship, or thoughts about others and the self). Via the water mirror children will be able to process their complex feelings by transferring them to the image, while they also gain a level of consciousness regarding their own thoughts.

Understanding one's own feelings and gaining overall self-awareness

Understanding of one's own feelings means getting to know one's inner world, one's own internal and external relationships; this knowledge comes with the widening of the mind and the growing collection of personal experiences. The creation of scenes, acting out, and collecting objects for personal use translates children's inner, personal experience into a concrete, three-dimensional form. As a picture, the objects, stories, and scenes created during play express feelings, emotions, and conflicts that might not have verbal language. Children who use objects in their play may often experience a sense of movement and progression by representing their own feminine and masculine power. While the calming effect of natural water and its environment will automatically calm the mind, the vegetation, mud, and natural water will also symbolically tame anger and frustration, as it will hide, bury, wash out, and take away the unwanted thoughts and feelings, therefore helping children to come to terms with their own feelings and balance their emotional state.

MOBILE OF FAVOURITE WATER SCHOOL OBJECTS

Children love collecting objects when in natural environments; they touch and observe things and 'taking a piece' of the nature is important for their memories, for the ability to link and belong. This, therefore, is an inevitable part of their internalisation process. Objects can physically link children to their experiences and feelings, which helps them in the process of acceptance when their body changes. Making a mobile means displaying treasure (mental rather than physical value) – for them, as well as for the special appreciation and reassurance of others. Making a mobile can be carried out by the children without prompting, but it can also serve as a part of a thematic learning process, discovering differences or similarities, for example in the shape of the body, surface, and colour of the skin.

USE STICKS TO CREATE A CHILD'S FAMILY

Using sticks to create puppets and story characters will enable to the children to personalise their understanding of stories, events, and human relationships. The children will be able to visualise the stories when creating or using the stick figures and by projecting feelings onto the objects their ability to process feelings will grow radically.

THE STICK ME: GETTING TO KNOW THE SELF

By making a timeline showing the different events in children's lives – making an animated version of the story about a stick family, taking a video of the children playing and speaking, and by using children's own images (drawings and photos) – the children can have a safe medium to communicate feelings and thoughts about their family relationships and home life.

OUR PEBBLE MAN: GETTING TO KNOW
THE ROOTS OF SELF

Children can make a 'nursery Pebble Man' that they can take home. The following day the children can describe the time Pebble Man spent in their homes to their peers; this enables them to talk about their own family lives.

Make a family tree – include the Pebble Man – for the children from sticks and photos. Try to create faces and facial expressions using the sticks to personalise each child's own stick men.

BUILD YOUR SANDMAN AND HIS HOUSE: GETTING TO
KNOW OTHERS, AND THE SELF IN RELATION TO OTHERS

Sand is a regularly used healing tool for its unique characteristics as a medium for thoughts: it is open-ended and has no right or wrong way to be used, giving freedom of play and expression; it is natural, with a powerful connection to our environment; it is easy and safe to manipulate; and it invites and permits users to engage at their own level. Piaget (1945) stated that children have an inner drive to build an understanding of their world as they explore and interact with natural materials. The rich Water School environment encourages children to exercise their freedom to play by having access to its vast array of resources, so children's concepts about how the world works are built gradually and become increasingly complex. Sand is a plentiful resource in Water School, and it can act as a canvas or material for creative work; it can be a background or a tool at the same time. By using sand to create a character and its environment and its world, children gain a different perspective on the meaning of being, in relation to themselves and others.

SECRET PLACE – THE ABILITY TO PROCESS FEELINGS

One of the regularly noticeable schemas is enveloping or containing, which often means children will hide away or cover themselves up. (For more information on schemas see p. 81.) In the natural environment of Water School children will have a range of materials, a variety of different colours, textures, weights, or temperatures to touch, discover, and play with, to support their enveloping schema play. The water and the surrounding natural resources have the ability to transform and disguise, and having legs and hands hidden under the water provides children with the unique experience of instant, visible, reversible transformation, that will still allow one to see what's underneath. Encouraging and permitting children to find a quiet area (a secret place) and experience how water changes things will help the further understanding of concepts like the 'object permanence' in a real-life situation. Having a secretive, undisturbed – almost magical – place to be assists children in developing an ability to process their life events, enabling them to work through problems without it resulting in emotional difficulties.

Physical well-being

Early years physical development is the process of gaining physical well-being for the developing self, which assists with:

- becoming comfortable with the physical self within the surrounding world by moving in different ways;
- gaining strength, stamina, and balance.

This process is not simply about getting stronger, but learning about and acceptance of the physical self – the body – in relation to others and the environment. Water play encourages the children to explore their own physical self. They develop eye/hand coordination through pouring, squeezing, stirring, painting, scrubbing, and squirting. Children strengthen their gross motor skills by running, dodging water drops, and hopping through a sprinkler. They widen their sensory experiences as they put their hands in different textures (gritty, squishy and slimy) and different temperatures, (warm, cool and cold) (Hendrick, 1998). Water School also stimulates the educators to trust children to take managed risks, supporting them to learn life skills.

Dig a channel, make a dam

Digging channels and making dams to manipulate the water will help children to understand how to transform the physical existence, and how everything is limited by different things, objects, or life forms. Children who understand the limitations of the physical world are more likely to accept and adapt to new situations in their everyday lives. The water is a great environment in which to learn about the physical self, as it is limiting the body's strength and changing the experience of body weight, while still allowing freedom.

Build a boat

Construction is an activity that helps the development of physical abilities (strength, fine motor skills, gross motor skills), as well as the understanding of physical characteristics (weight, size, length, depth, colour, appearance).

Using mud as glue and building material, designing

Making little models, creating a small imaginary world, creating figurines and equipment, making a Drip House by scooping up handfuls of wet, dripping mud and by repeating to create Drip City, are all activities that will help children to understand themselves and their environment, and make sense of their own place within it.

Mud for physical needs

Using mud as plaster to create tiles and plaques will highlight the more practical uses of mud, generating a deeper understanding of physical needs, for example building houses to live in. Performing necessary exercises through mud (jumping, walking, digging, and lifting) strengthens children's stamina and physical abilities. Creating mud puddles or mini ponds to jump in will help children to understand their own body (how we get tired, why we need exercise, why we need sleep, why it is important to look after the body).

Water School resources to aid movement

Sticks, pebbles, driftwood, and mud all contribute to the physical activities set for the children within Water School: trying to copy the movements of *Stick Man* from Julia Donaldson's story (e.g. scratch, scrape, wiggle, jiggle, poke, shove, nudge, hop, jump); exploring with the children what words can be used to describe movements; observing animals as they use sticks and try to mimic their movements (e.g. building nests) to develop directionality and body image; using large sticks for den-building, to encourage gross motor development, hand-eye coordination, and laterality; providing opportunities for weaving to develop fine motor skills.

Mud and water as a sensory experience

Sensory experiences aid physical well-being. Exploring what mud and water smells like, what it feels like, what it looks like – this helps children to become confident about their own bodies and feelings, thus developing their ability to express their own views. Mud is an open-ended material and it can meet the needs and interests of different children from different age groups. Mud is a sensory art medium, and its limitless free supply allows children to make mistakes without the consequences of those in conventional art programmes: a mud-picture painted in the soil or sand can be easily wiped and recreated. Children can experience creating with different tools, chosen by them (leaves, sticks, pebbles, their own hands).

Communication and social connections

The ability to communicate is the core of all social interactions and it is one of the essential skills children need to have. The children develop their communication by being motivated, by being provided with reasons and opportunities to do so. The Water School environment can be an extremely motivational place for developing communication skills and to stimulate their use, as children must first experience the desire to express their thoughts, ideas, intentions, and emotions. The Water School environment has the relaxing background sound of water – less of a distraction than the traditional classroom. Some children, especially boys, seem to become more communicative and more vocal when they are engaged in active learning. The water environment allows for the different learners to find their own motivation, from the calm to the energetic. This type of play – where children explore natural materials such as wood, sand, water, and stones – stimulates their sense of touch and sound, so they begin to notice the different feel of things – wet, sticky, muddy – and hear how things make different sounds: the 'whoosh' sound of water, the splash of puddles, the clunk of pebbles, the dripping of rain, the lapping or roaring of the waves, and the bubbling of the flowing river. These types of sounds help children to understand the difference between different sounds, and such auditory experiences also improve their mood and sleep, calm down their nervous system, and help fight against stress and emotional difficulties. When children play water games that are initiated and led by them, they use and learn language naturally. Specially used Water School words such as flow, drip, funnel, dam, surface, submerge, whip, float, and strain enrich the young children's growing vocabulary and allow them to express themselves more explicitly about their immediate experiences, so this will motivate them to describe their world with various expressions elsewhere as well as in Water School. Positional language (under, on, in, above, next to, within) and expressive words for comparison (lighter, first, middle, larger, smaller) emerge automatically from water-play experiences. Children who have difficulties (special learning needs, English as a second language) will benefit from the natural interaction when working together side by side with others. Children's Water School play can also be incorporated into their written communication learning by finding age-appropriate ways of recording.

Water book

Children can paint the story of their Water School day with water on wooden surfaces and sanded spaces. Together they can use the water to create a 'book' or a 'written' report and, using skills such as remembering, working together, and finding words to describe experiences. They also learn to see themselves from the view of others and learn to appreciate the feelings and thoughts of their peers; they will gain an understanding of time – past and future – by creating their own stories woven into those of others. Made with water, the creations will dry up without damaging or changing the environment.

The weather forecast team

As children make and check their own predictions, they can be encouraged to record them. While working together, listening, and taking turns in this way, children can also learn that print will function to help people to remember or to convey information. The 'printing' process will also be useful in labelling things (liked, disliked, memorable) or telling the story of a sequence of steps (e.g. what happened when the rain did arrive, what sound the river made when windy, why we thought there would be a storm).

Project managers

Natural materials and the natural environment can act as community builders when the children use them to plan and carry out projects together. Creating a wormery or a bug hotel, approaching the Water School environment to investigate which creatures live there, talking about conservation, homing animals, and sustaining life will help the children in building a real, meaningful sense of community.

The little scientists

Advancing language skills via science projects is an interesting, engaging way of learning new words and expressions. With its unique properties, water play usually leads children to ask about what they are experiencing (often for the first time): How does the river keep the wood on its surface? Can it be changed? Why does water flow that way? Children's innate curiosity will lead to a desire to experiment, which will stimulate further curiosity and provoke additional questions. Children will test and challenge their own and others' knowledge and engage in creative thinking as they explore the unique characteristics of natural water, from its colour, texture, and temperature to its properties: to float, sink, cover, show, highlight, and change objects and living beings. The children will automatically reach conclusions based on their experiences, therefore the concepts they build and learn will be understood by them on a deeper level (as they try and test them). Children become active members of their social and learning community by studying the Water School environment together: learning about nature and its energetic forces, about sustainability, about the characteristics and states of different physical matters, about ecological and physical laws, based on their repeated scientific experiments and observations.

Marks: creating an individual imprint and understanding signs, symbols, and feelings

According to many researchers (Grandin, 2005; Verstegen, 2005), educators, and my own experience, children are visual-based thinkers with active and vivid imaginations, based on their experiences of growing up. Children are often observed building on the concrete sensory events from their life and their experiences are worked into various images of their artistic process. Children's thinking is visually, metaphorically, and emotionally driven, rather than logical. They are emotional thinkers who learn to become engaged with the very core of their world, so they can grow into radical thinkers who challenge and change the key beliefs they all originally have about the way the world is – and should be. Simply by recognising similarities and common traits, children have a unique ability to make connections between things that may not seem logical to the adult brain. A child's brain senses images and scenes, and translates these experiences into metaphors. Therefore, when making marks to process their own experiences, children are likely to use metaphors. Metaphorical play – children pretending that one object is another – is a way of making sense of the world around them.

Found object statues

Collecting odd objects from the Water School environment and using them to create statues enables the children to develop an understanding of the importance of keeping our natural environment clean, and making positive environmental marks as well as having great fun. It educates children in other learning areas: working together will develop their social skills; planning/sectioning off areas will help their understanding of the world; they will develop their communication abilities while negotiating.

Water spirit

Children can create underwater images with pebbles and/or other natural resources. While learning about different materials (what sinks, what floats) the children will also develop a closer relationship with nature by giving it a personality with a name and characteristics.

Message in a bottle

Children develop a greater understanding of the meaning of words and how they can convey meaning and connect people by sending a message in a bottle. Instead of using glass or plastic bottles and affecting the environment, children can work out different ways to make the message travel, for example making a leaf boat or putting a miniature message in a walnut shell.

Shadows underneath

By observing the shadows underneath created by different things on the surface and above the water, children will develop an eye for detail, their observation skills will advance, and by describing what they see their vocabulary will widen. It will help children to understand that things leave a mark, and marks have a meaning.

Car tracks and fairy stories in damp sand

Different types of graphic symbol systems such as drawing, painting, and scribbling provide children with their basic understanding of making an enduring, material, and transmittable sum of their thoughts, therefore the majority of young children have a strong desire to make marks. This is their way to process the events of their lives and to establish how relating to these events makes sense of the world in which they live. When children are encouraged to talk about, share, and revisit their experiences they become aware of different possibilities for representation of their own lives. Creating car tracks, picturing fairy stories, making shopping lists . . . there are many variations when using the beach or riverbank sand as a canvas.

Masks: marks of self within the environment

Children can experience mark-making in a different way when creating natural masks to camouflage themselves and blend in with the environment. Being under water is a great way to observe how different things affect each other in the world, and how the moving water changes the appearance of things. Children will learn how to communicate their inner world, how to make their own marks, by the experience of hiding themselves and by observing how animals and plants hide in nature, which is a good way to identify feelings that are hidden and have formed into a mask. Marks of one's inner world will help the children to process their thoughts and feelings effectively and to deal with difficulties in their lives.

Pattern hunting with magnifying glasses

The development of mark-making starts from birth, when children start to observe the world around them. They study the details of their surroundings to form a complete picture. Encouraging children to actively look for details, and to notice and compare things will assist their learning in later life. Children can experience how water magnifies, and using magnifying glasses will inspire and motivate them to carry out their own hunting projects.

Plant marks

Children will benefit greatly from being given the opportunity and the trust to manipulate their environment. They can colour the water with natural dyes such as plants, berries, and herbs and while learning about the importance of marks, they also develop an artistic view and gain a basic understanding of sustainability.

Expression and creativity

The Water School environment with its ongoing changes is an engaging place for children as they have an innate drive and passion to explore their surroundings, motivating them to follow their ideas, which will then lead to even more exploration. Creativity is the conscious and unconscious process of following IDEAS. This process consists of five steps:

1   Interest/exploration: children show an interest and follow their interest through exploring their surroundings.
2   Discovery and investigation: children discover things (concepts, objects, others, relationships etc.) and investigate, examining their discoveries.
3   Event conclusion: children will arrive at a conclusion in the form of stating their thoughts, feelings, opinions.
4   Affirming and advocating: children will share the conclusion of their thinking with others.
5   Switching to new: as their new knowledge generates more interest and inspires new ideas, children will use their new knowledge to 'switch back' to 'interest mode' and explore further.

The pedagogical delivery methods of Water School follow a learning environment that not only excites and interests the children in new and engaging investigations and experiments, but through the individual and collaborative discoveries it also deepens children's knowledge and further develops their creative thinking for future success in life. As children are sensory learners, their creativity is sparked by highly sensory environments, such as Water School, where the different shades of light, the different textures and temperatures, the various colours, and interesting smells will encourage and help children to be at one with nature on their own level, following their own interests, so they can immerse themselves in a sensory experience.

Nature-colour-copying

Children can try to create different shades of colours as seen in nature, simply by using water, earth, sand, and plants. This will provide the children with an exceptional variety of colours from rich yellow, through vibrant green, to deep brown. When creating detailed visual art and expressing thoughts within the deep connection to nature, children will understand further the purpose of resources, while also developing meticulous attention to detail.

Water School sculptures and nature art gallery

While sludge may not sound the most inviting art material, creating drip sludge sculptures provides the children with tremendous fun and many learning opportunities. Manipulating, embellishing, sticking, balancing, transforming, and shaping the material, while incorporating other materials, will require creative and cognitive thinking on a high level, including artistic skills and mathematical knowledge. Organising a mud art gallery in the Water School environment will develop children's social skills: they learn to share, they learn to give and take praise, and they develop early public responsibility (keeping nature clean, looking after living beings etc.).

Water theatre

Creating and designing a small world by using sticks and pebbles to build habitats for small stick, pebble, or clay characters will be an enjoyable, creative activity for children. Children can organise a puppet show based on their own stories, and their own musical instruments can turn their show into theatre. Using stick-drums and engaging in rhythmic activities can jazz up their theatre and by inviting guests they can raise money to plant trees and save wetlands. The ability to work together effectively as part of a team is a key skill for children's lives.

Water kitchen

Studies – even from the late nineteenth century – have shown the direct relationship between role play and children's mental and emotional well-being and their behavioural development. In the late 1600s John Locke, a British philosopher, popularised the notion that toys helped the learning process, and by the end of the 1700s there were educational toys for many different subject areas (Smith, 2005). In the 1800s, children did have free, unstructured time – even if only rarely; they would play games using whittled or corn husk toys.

In Water School every aspect of role play in the kitchen can be easily managed, as everything can act as part of a domestic area: sticks as wooden spoons; mud, water, and earth as ingredients; shells and small pebbles as spices; leaves and seaweed as herbs; and pieces of wood as pots and pans. While pretending within the safe frame of play, children can test theories they witness around them: they can practise their language knowledge to negotiate, they can observe the emotions of themselves and others, and they can take risks without serious consequences.

Jewellery making

Children's artistic talents can be drawn upon in the natural environment through jewellery making. The children can collect stones, pebbles, shells, foliage, and fallen leaves to create a visual representation of their specially designed jewellery. The process of creating allows children a wholly sensory experience, developing their planning, collaborating, and decision-making skills, and learning to be patient.

Watersounds: the water band

Listening to, differentiating, and comparing sounds encourages children's listening skills and stimulates speaking. Going on a sound hunt, guessing the sound, and copying sounds are beneficial games for children to develop their early literacy skills. Research shows (Dodd and Gillon, 2001; Ehri, 2004) that children need a good understanding of sounds prior to developing a phonological awareness and clear speech. Children can make music by manipulating the water with different tools such as throwing in stones, splashing with sticks, dripping from hands, pouring from shell containers, and creating waves.

Understanding and creating concepts, logical, and mathematical meaning-making

Studying nature is the best way for children to understand the world they live in, to find out how the world works, how they can fit in and what their personal aim and purpose is. Learning about the Water School environment using the simplest actions (looking, seeing, touching, holding, and smelling) will help children to understand more complex concepts later in life. As they listen or talk to educators and parents about their experiences in Water School, they gain additional information in relation to their own past, family history, neighbourhood, and their broader environment, slowly developing their own life story, recognising the role of technology in the universe, and building an awareness of the world.

Water School science

All materials in the Water School environment can be subjects of scientific investigations: the elements, solids, solvents, solutions, the components of mud in various environments, changes to materials in the process of freezing or melting, exploring volume, observing cause and effect, testing simple hypotheses as materials are added and taken away. Encourage children to collect different sticks from a local field / park, measure their length/width and weight, make number charts using sticks, and create a nature clock using sticks to represent time which will all expand their developing mathematical knowledge.

Water hunt

Searching for different forms of water, organising water-foraging trips in different seasons, and investigating where water collects in the natural environment will help children to understand physical concepts such as changes in substance, quantity, and quality, and will also provide them with a wealth of knowledge about the passing of time and seasonal differences (which ultimately helps them to accept changes in their own lives).

Water mapping

Finding all the wet places nearby and creating a map showing the journey that the children take to find them will help the children to build knowledge of their local area. This helps them to be more independent and safe, while also developing their memory.

The life of water

While the children play, explain and inspire them to think about where water comes from, how humans and animals use water, where water can be found; think about why things float, test and measure different materials; explore how water has been used throughout human history; go on archaeology trips (dig holes and see if water-related objects can be found underground), observe water found in different places.

Waterworld

Observe 'live' water: what lives in water and how humans relate to the underwater world. Create a miniature underwater world and create habitats; using commentary, encourage the children to express their thoughts about their creations. The children will develop a wider vocabulary, an ability to describe and reason, and an understanding of relationships between things, while also being able to create, manipulate, and direct.

Developing and teaching children in Water School

The natural environment is one of the most enabling places to develop children's understanding of their world. Their creative processes, their IDEAS, and their learning happen immediately due to being constantly encouraged, together with being given choices, so their learning is active due to being purposeful and happy. In the Water School environment children make choices with what nature offers to them; the adults need to wait and observe what the children choose to do. Nature's offer is exactly right for the children in their early years, as it is:

- light but not too bright
- organised but not clinical
- clean but not sterile
- inviting – not overwhelming or cluttered
- noisy but calm
- open but offers smaller (hiding) places.

The Water School learning process is like its main feature – natural water: it is constant, immediate, flowing, changing, active, moving, and sensitive to impact. It automatically assists educators in the process of forming a child-focused teaching approach: the MOTIVE (which describes the required characteristics of the educators) kept in motion and put into practice via the teaching method, the MOTORS.

MOTIVE describes the correct approach of the Water School educator:

Meaningful time: the sensitive, relaxed practitioner is giving time to children so they can develop an idea or react to one, being with them, next to them, awaiting their answer. This will help them to trust their intuition and instinct as well as to build relationships with others.

Observing with awe and enchantment: the enthusiastic practitioner displays awe and enchantment that will keep children interested and motivated. Modelled by the adults around them, children will allow themselves to appreciate their environment.

Teaching by reflection: the reflective practitioner commentates rather than comments on what children do, so their play processes will be lifted from the unconscious to the conscious level. The children will gain an understanding about themselves that enables them to own and direct their individual learning.

Influential purpose: the motivated practitioner provides children with the opportunity to develop their own ideas and work in accordance with their own plans and strategies. The children will repeatedly focus and try to complete tasks (set for themselves) so they will overcome barriers and truly embrace success.

'V's interaction: the interacting, interested practitioner uses vivid, vital, and valid communication and their modelling encourages children to use verbal and non-verbal communication. Vivid communication means the educators react at the time of the children's action, with important (vital) and relevant (valid) information.

Extemporary planning: the up-to-date practitioner understands that while planning itself suggests being prepared in advance, planning for being extemporary means that the educators are prepared to act as very vigilant observers and allow the children to follow their own agenda, their own immediate planning – the children impact, the educators react, and together they co-act.

When teaching with MOTIVE, educators will have reasons for doing things with the children, who will then cause or be a reason for the educators to constantly do something new only in order to move the children forward, which will be the MOTORS of the education:

Muddle: the educator observes the children's impulses in a skilful, vigilant, and thorough way, getting to know the children's individual way of thinking.

Organisation: the educator guides the children in the collection and organisation of thoughts and ideas.

Turbulence: the educator responds immediately, accordingly, only as needed to answer the children's questions and to move the thought process forward toward active learning.

Occurrence of conclusions: the educator summarises children's actions via commentating and reflecting to help the children understand their own learning process.

Reaction: the educator teaches children by reacting to – NOT CORRECTING – their experiences, and acknowledges the appearance of impulses.

Silence: the educator accepts the children's process (for what it is, without expectations and pre-determined aims), allowing the process to flow and ensuring time and silence to deepen the learning.

In this way of teaching, the observation of the individual child's learning is the key. Even though the development areas are important, looking at individual developmental milestones (in the context of significant individual achievements, small steps of development) gives a clearer view of each child; it informs the educators precisely about the child's stage of growing. While in most areas children typically develop through certain steps in certain windows of time, as each child is unique, milestones are more individual to the child. In the Water School programme, milestones – different from the classic meaning (abilities that are achieved by most children by a certain age) – indicate *turning points* or *landmark* occasions in the child's learning. Developmental milestones can involve physical, social, emotional, cognitive and communication, artistic, or any skills that are important for the children themselves. When looking at milestones and connecting them, educators gain an insight to the children's learning story, where knowledge (in its classic, educational meaning) is additional detail, with the main focus being on the journey the children are going through.

Milestone observation

Observing children's milestones cannot be carried out by completing tick lists or prepared forms. Milestone observation requires the professional educator/parent to know the child's actual developmental stage, preferred activities, abilities, skills, likes, and dislikes in detail. This type of observation by a vigilant adult will show development not as a simple linear chart, as the child learns something new every day and their acquired skills will assist them in almost all of the learning areas. For example, a child who walks to the river and places his hands into the water for the first time individually and says, 'It's icy cold,' to a peer, demonstrates a whole array of skills by this simple act: the child shows confidence to approach the river (emotional development, physical development); he shows an emerging need to communicate his own observation (social development); he demonstrates his level of vocabulary and descriptive language (communication); he displays an understanding of his environment (understanding of the world); while also showing an overall curiosity and ability to use existing knowledge and make links. When carrying out a milestone-observation in Water School, educators will answer simple questions from the observed child's point of view:

- What is the child doing?
- How does the child relate to the environment?
- How long is the child occupied with the activity?
- Does the child link many activities or focus on one in particular?

- What skills does the child use/display?
- Has the child been observed doing this before (how, when)?
- Is the child alone or in a small/large group? How does the child relate to others in the environment?

The milestone observation can be recorded as answers to the questions or as an anecdotal description, which over time can form the child's learning story. This type of recording creates a story told by the children, rather than directed by the observer.

Schemas in Water School

One of the ways in which children build up their own understanding of their world is schematic learning. Young children can often be observed displaying repeated patterns of behaviour – called schemas – that assist children in the exploration and expression of their developing ideas and thoughts, and in their play and growing knowledge. Repetitive actions of schematic play allow children to gradually construct an understanding and meaning of what happens in their world and how they relate to it. Water School is a perfect place for the children to deepen and extend their schematic play, as the environment and its resources will naturally offer opportunities stemming from the repetitive, orderly, and schematic characteristics of nature.

Rotation	Children will often be fascinated with the spinning movement, therefore objects rolled by the water will entertain these children and help them learn.
Trajectory	Some children who are fascinated with movement prefer straight movements and long lines. They will really enjoy playing with the flowing water, studying the rolling stones or swimming fish.
Positioning	Some children will benefit from being given the opportunity to place objects in different positions – next, over, under – and the natural environment will provide them with many opportunities to do so. Patterns of behaviour for this schema can include a general interest in where things are.
Orientation	Some children will observe things from different angles. The water surface is a perfect 'magic mirror' to study the self-image, reflections of the environment, or portraits of others from a changed view.
Connection	Some children will enjoy collecting things from the environment – pebbles, shells, driftwood, sticks, leaves, feathers etc. – and working on different ways to group or link them will help their learning.
Transporting	Water is a great thing to carry for children who learn by this schema, as they will be able to easily manipulate the amount of water, as well as select natural objects according to their own abilities. This will also allow children to challenge themselves at their own natural pace.
Transforming	Children who learn by manipulating textures – mixing and changing things – can find plenty of resources to cater naturally for their

own learning: mud, water, sand, earth, sticks, and natural hollows and coves. This schema can be observed when children like to explore and see changes.

Enclosure   Some children learn by emptying and refilling holes, and wrapping objects so that they are contained inside. Water is a perfect medium to contain and cover any object, while the Water School environment has natural places to confine objects and the self.

Enveloping   Children often like to enclose or contain themselves, to wrap and cover things. In Water School the water and the mud are all natural 'containers' for the children's hands and feet.

The Water School environment will allow children to change and adapt their schematic behaviour according to their own learning rhythm, but Water School activities can also be adapted to support schematic learners. Traditional early years activities can be carried out with resources found in the natural environment.

Children's developing brains create thousands of links between its cells every hour, stimulated by experiencing the world around them. Newly formed links are fragile and temporary; children's practice and repetition activities make them strong and permanent. Duplicating and replaying the same situations, the same efforts, and the same operations within many different situations, environments, and with a wide selection of resources, transforms the tenuous neural pathways; via this process play activities will become memories and experiences, and the experiences gradually grow into a lifelong knowledge. Improved understanding of the schemas' role in Water School can influence the educators' approach to children's learning, which will become child-led and personally tailored.

Children with difficulties in Water School

Children with special educational needs

Creating a safe, enclosed outdoor play space nearby where children can relax and maybe even learn, while also enjoying the enhanced therapeutic benefits of fresh air and nature, should be provided for all children, as they will sleep better, play better, and even eat better. For children with special educational needs, however, the multisensory, still, calming outdoor environment is even more important than for their neuro-typical peers.

THE ORDERLY CHANGE VEHICLE

For children who have severe, profound, and/or multiple learning difficulties, the Water School environment provides the ideal vehicle for following a sensory curriculum. It is a great opportunity for educators and children to use the natural environment to teach these children about themselves, each other, and the natural world, which belongs to them and in which they live. The water, with its calming characteristics and natural power, reduces the challenge for children of having to change their natural attitude toward learning – as is often required in the classroom – so the perceived complications of exposing such vulnerable children to the elements is outweighed by the benefits

Table 4.1 Schemas in Water School

Activity	Enclosure, containing, enveloping	Transporting, positioning	Rotation	Trajectory	Transformation	Connection
Mud or sludge painting	Borders, covering	Taking mud paint to different places	Stirring mud paint	Creating lines	Mixing, diluting	Patterns, symmetry
Outdoor cooking	Food in pots. Wrapping potato in foil to cook, stuffing edible leaves. Putting things away.	Making a fire	Stirring, whisking, mixing, rolling out pastry	Collecting right sized sticks for fire	Cutting up ingredients, using pestle and mortar, how water evaporates	Sequence in recipes
Driftwood as building blocks and woodwork	Collecting, sorting, grouping driftwood	Models with wheels	Floating driftwood constructions	Creating long lines of driftwood, comparison, hammering	Cutting up driftwood, building and demolishing towers	Building with driftwood, creating nuts and bolts
Water play	Washing things, filling up bottles, pipes, and funnels, making boats, blow bubbles	Making boats, floating	Creating watermills	Pouring, guttering	Dying water with berries, stirring up waterbed	Building bridges
Sand (wet and dry)	Covering with sand, treasure hunt	Studying how water transports sand	Creating mills	Funnels, waterways, digging	Wetting and drying out sand, covering with sand	Sandcastle, filling things, building funnels, waterways
Pebble play as small world	Creating hides, homes with pebble people	Mimicking real world events with pebbles	Studying pebbles in the flowing water	Pebble people Olympic races, pebble people measurements	Painting pebbles to represent changes, differences in children's physique	Making houses with clay/mud as natural cement
Sound and natural music	Creating natural listening tubes by rolling up leaves	Echo, studying how voice travels	Natural chants, drumming, ring games	Recording natural sound, listening, imitating	Making natural xylophone, studying how voice changes near water	Percussion, sound copying games, sounds of water

achieved. Because the natural environment is changing constantly, children automatically become more accepting of change (which children with special educational needs often struggle with); they grow to be more comfortable and confident when outdoors. The instant change differentiates Water School from Forest School, and this rapidly changing environment is what makes Water School a successful learning space for children with difficulties. Through this Orderly Change Vehicle children develop a sense of joy and ownership as, unlike a structured indoor classroom, the water environment has no expectations, with no particular way to approach it; it is free and appropriate for all but still provides a level of order, balance, and routine.

Children who have autistic spectrum disorder, Asperger's syndrome, or attention deficit hyperactivity disorder (ADHD) are typically locked into their own world, following their repetitive mode of behaviour, displaying only a small range of familiar reactions, and being transported to an alien environment such as the riverside could be unsettling, with its lack of security, familiarity, and routine. However, pushing the boundaries of their own worlds is what moves their learning forward. With Water School's carefully tailored experiences, close supervision, and one-to-one support of a familiar adult, these children will be able to embrace the Water School environment in order to learn about their environment and themselves in relation to the environment. Through the Orderly Change Vehicle their skills, abilities, and likes are transferable, which will motivate them to become more and more accepting in other areas of their lives. The working of the Orderly Change Vehicle of the Water School environment builds on the observed cycle-like change, regularity, and patternedness of nature that humans can automatically sense and become drawn to. For example children can observe and learn that there will be water in Water School, it will be deep, coloured, somewhat cold and moving, but its depth, exact colour, temperature, and surface will almost always be completely different. This is the ideal vehicle to teach children with special educational needs to differentiate between static and moving, between permanent and changing things in their environment and therefore in their lives.

Children with special educational needs learn to develop a personal connection with nature and their own immediate environment, so they gain a more meaningful and responsive relationship to it. This relationship and the ability to form the relationship can then be used in educational applications, and it can also foster respect and an ability to care for the environment. All types of Water School environments have unique and varied potential as an opportunity for learning, through exploration and experimentation with the materials found there each time the area is visited. The benefits of working alongside others, negotiating the different problems occurring when the area is visited at different times (caused by time, weather, seasonal changes etc.), recognising how to make ideas come to fruition in the changing environment will help children to overcome more easily the problems in other areas of their lives.

CASE STUDY

In the Olympus KeyMed day nursery in Southend the educators cared for a four-year-old child with ADHD and English as a second language. The child appeared to have a lack of attention, found it hard to concentrate for long periods of time, and he almost never engaged with group activities in the classroom. The child was rarely observed to play with anyone other than two selected peers; they were occupied with one type of high-energy game, but the ADHD child was only required to run around and display loud noises. During the Water School session the child was taken to the local beach in a small group, alongside two children whom the child had never been seen to communicate or play with previously. The Water School sessions that the ADHD child took part in were partially structured, and the free-play section of the session had a determined aim: finding a crab. During the sessions the ADHD child was observed to concentrate on one activity for about one hour; he appeared to be focused and driven; he negotiated his ideas with his peers; he showed an ability to accept the opinion of others; and also shared joy and pride. The activity showed a balanced mixture of order and surprise, and the child displayed an age-appropriate level of knowledge, and an ability to accept change and follow instructions. In the meantime he learnt about environmental management, the flora/fauna of the local beach, and he even demonstrated the right level of negotiation when convincing his shyer peers to attend the slippery sea vegetation.

Play therapy in Water School

Water is a natural environment for humans from their first moment of life. Water is extremely important for the human body and soul, internally and externally, which is the main reason why traditional therapies use water in its different forms to heal the human physique and mind. Natural water and its environment are in themselves therapeutic, as nature allows humans to reconnect with their own inner world. Water has the ability to replace a communication context when children face difficulties in expressing their thoughts. Water is an active medium that can be mixed with many other materials and with its easily formable, manageable characteristic, children can manipulate water, mud, and sand to foster their connection to the power of imagination. Water and water-related materials form a universal language with which to make meaning.

Children have an even closer bond to the water–life experience than mature adults. Children naturally use the water's power – mentally and physically – and are much more open to receive the calming and deepening effect of various forms of natural water, such as rain, rivers, and sea. Children often have an inbuilt affinity to choose water as the environment for their natural expression and play. This natural means of expression is used as a therapeutic method to assist children in coping with troubles and trauma in their life, as it releases stress and hosts a self-healing process. Children who have an understanding level of at least a normal three-year-old will be able to work on their own problems such as being distraught due to family problems (e.g. parental divorce, sibling rivalry), displaying aggressive or cruel behaviour, being socially underdeveloped, victims of child abuse, or children whose disability is a source of anxiety or emotional turmoil. The healing method of play therapy builds on allowing the child to manipulate the world on a smaller scale, something that, for different reasons, the child is often unable to do in their everyday environment.

In a traditional therapy room children play with specially selected materials under the guidance of a person who reacts in a designated manner; the child plays out his/her feelings, bringing these hidden emotions to the surface where s/he can face them and cope with them. In its most non-directive form, the therapist is unconditionally accepting of anything the child might say or do, which develops a relaxed atmosphere.

According to some experienced therapists (Stevens, 2003; Gronning *et al.*, 2007), water may represent the 'mother figure' and significant relationships in children's symbolic play. The size of the water drawn/painted/represented/mentioned by the children can indicate the importance of the relationship. The colour of the water, its other characteristics, the flora and fauna living in it, are all indicators and marks of the child's inner world.

In Water School the basics of play therapy gain new meaning by the changed environment. Children still symbolically express their inner voice, but the tools are different. In Water School, children can experience – as they do in the therapy room – the feeling of responsibility, being able to manipulate tools to express and to process their thoughts, and the therapist is capable of providing boundaries through the environment. Within play therapy in Water School the practitioner offers children a safe place to play out their thoughts, feelings, and problems. The therapist still provides tools that encourage 'fantasy play', such as clay, sand, water, drawing materials, and puppets – all made from natural materials that enable children to act out real-life scenarios. The therapist builds warm and supportive relationships with the children, thereby encouraging them to open up through the symbolic language of play. During the therapy session the few limits are easy to set (playing with anything they like, unless they hurt the environment and its elements) and the children are given complete freedom to control their actions in play, empowering them to indicate the source of their inner emotional disturbance via their behaviour in the play. Water School naturally helps the therapist to use appropriate techniques to help the children develop coping mechanisms for use in their real lives.

Various tools can be used within Water School to provide therapeutic play opportunities for children in need. The play therapy toolkit consists of techniques, methods, and resources used by practitioners during sessions, adapted to situations and difficulties that arise.

- *Creative visualisation*: the creative visualisation technique usually takes the children into an imaginative safe place, and the Water School environment automatically creates the physical frame to work with.
- *Art*: vegetation, berries, and flowers are perfect to colour and create with, while any surface can be used as a canvas.
- *Storytelling*: stories can be told in any environment, however using natural settings with flora and fauna can set the basic scene of stories, and can provide an exciting background and a large variety of characters, both real and imaginary.
- *Sandtray and miniatures*: vegetation, pebbles, stones, shells, driftwood, and found objects provide the perfect selection of figurines while the shore, bank, or beach act as natural sandtrays.
- *Music*: natural sounds (wind, flowing river, waves, rain etc.) provide natural rhythm, while it is also simple to use pieces of wood or pebbles as natural instruments.
- *Dance and movement*: play therapy builds on children's natural affinity with water and ability to move freely, and the water encourages children to follow their own natural flow.
- *Puppets and mask*: natural objects are perfect for making dramatic and diverse masks and puppets, while the appearance and actions of the living beings in the

water environment naturally lend themselves to imaginative play and the transference of emotions.

- *Clay*: mud and earth can always be found in the Water School environment and provide an unlimited medium for the children to freely manipulate.

THE WATER CIRCLE

The circle is an extremely powerful symbol: it is closed yet infinite; it is defined yet soft; it can be all one or divided; and often different parts of the personality can be brought into its creation as it can be easily sectioned. Therefore, it is widely used as a therapeutic tool. Levi and Klein (2000) believe that humans are born with the desire to look at circles; it is believed that this helps them bond with their primary caregiver. By softening all shapes and edges the water naturally assists human vision and the mind, which prefer to look at curved lines more than straight ones. Water softens all forms, so they are easier for the brain to process, as circular shapes look similar from all angles. The circle is also a representation of 'wholeness' or 'fullness'. By creating an image in a circular area sectioned off in the water or on the river bank, deep emotions are lifted into the field of view or 'awareness'. A circular shallow container is the perfect medium for creating a water circle, which can help children to visually express, experience and, therefore, process inner energies and what might be happening within the deepest parts of their 'self'. The activity of creating a circle can act as a vehicle for the mind to round the parts of the inner operating system so they might fit together into wholeness, and by acknowledging them visually, they will likely to begin to work in harmony in the children's lives.

The Water Circle provides important information about the children's psyche by the observers looking at any patterns or themes, any hot spots or ignored spots, parts competing for attention, colours used, or unique and different shapes within the children's creations.

WATER-PEBBLE STORYCRAFTING

Art and stories are very powerful tools of play therapy and water-pebble storycrafting combines the children's use of these tools. Although it seems to be directive, it is rather provocative and motivating. This tool consists of a simple sequence of actions that, if followed skilfully, encourages the children to tell their story with words or actions.

1   *Provocation (provocative action)*: the adult, situated next to the child, throws a pebble into the water as a provocative action.
2   *Observation and repetition*: the adult observes the child's reactions, and if the reaction is inactive with low energy, the adult repeats the action.
3   *Reflection by provocative questions*: the adult than reflects by asking questions to motivate the child to start a process (I wonder what happened to the pebble . . . What could happen if the pebble was alive? . . . What would the pebble say if it could speak? . . . What would the pebble feel?).
4   *Stimulation (prompting, inspiring, inciting action)*: the adult provides artistic Water School materials and starts to decorate a pebble to characterise it (for example by naming it, stating its characteristics).

5   *Creation of story by reflective summarising*: the adult summarises the child's story by reflecting on the child's actions and reactions, so the child's inner process is lifted into the conscious level of the mind.

SHELTER-PLANT-ANIMAL

Based on the well-known method of the House-Tree-Person drawing (Buck, 1948, 1981), the Shelter-Plant-Animal is a lively, child-friendly adaptation of the original psychological diagnostic tool, where the subject of the test receives a short, unclear instruction (the stimulus) to draw a house, a tree, and the figure of a person. Once done, the individual is asked to describe the picture. The method builds on the assumption that, when an individual is drawing, the inner world of the psyche is projected onto the page, therefore the subject's inner world can be investigated through the drawings. John Buck's method, which he originally based on the Goodenough scale of intellectual functioning, was developed in 1948 with its qualitative and quantitative measurements of intellectual ability, but it was criticised for having a weak validity. It is, however, concluded by many researchers (Koestler, 1964; Amabile, 1996; Andreasen, 2011) that the unconscious mind is activated by creative processes. It has also been observed how children engage with their own subconscious during their play, using different kinds of symbolism and metaphorical language, therefore engaging in a creative process represented by such strong symbols, the children are likely to communicate their feelings, thoughts, and/or difficulties.

The Shelter-Plant-Animal exercise consists of asking the children to observe the environment, select an animal of their choice (this can be assisted by drawings or photos from previous Water School sessions) and create a shelter for the animal with or from plants. The observer then draws information about the children's feelings/thoughts from the details of the children's creations, from the children's commentaries (if any), and from their general process of creating.

The power of the Shelter-Plant-Animal exercise rests on different factors:

- Creation is based on children's innate relation to nature and its elements, flora, and fauna.
- The exercise utilises the real and symbolic meaning and metaphoric aspects of houses/homes, the environment, and other living beings.
- The tangible nature of the process caters for a wider range of abilities (as opposed to drawing, which might make some children feel inadequate).

In the Water School therapy space the children can work through their problems that they would similarly tackle in the play therapy room:

- Representative and imaginary play: water is an excellent medium for imaginary play and for recreating one's inner world, as it can be easily manipulated.
- Control based play, self-management, and organisation: by separating objects, cleaning the water environment, and spotting similarities and differences children can demonstrate their need to feel in control and reduce chaos or stress in their lives.

- Confidence building: being able to hit/crush the water can be very powerful for children, who create mastery games to host the scenes they play out. The water can represent various environments, can lift, enhance, and clean things, as well as hide, transform, or make them muddy.
- Stress, frustration, and anger management: children can create games to release stress as the water is a perfect vehicle for high-energy and low-energy play; it can be easily manipulated and changed without causing a lasting effect.
- Self-soothing, relaxation, and calming: the sensory experience of water can have an extremely calming effect on children. Through its relaxing nature and its ability to act as a transporting vehicle between different parts of the world, it becomes a vehicle between the internal and external worlds, encouraging children to open up and talk more freely.
- Motivation: due to the large variety of sensory input, Water School – as a therapy environment – motivates children to relive and process previous life experiences.

Chapter 5

Health and safety in Water School

Introduction

This chapter will consider the health and safety aspects of the Water School programme, giving important information and practical advice to practitioners by pointing out basic health and safety rules, and the factors that can affect the delivery of the programme: weather and environmental changes. It will outline the health and safety policies and procedures that ensure the safe delivery of the programme.

An excellent Water School provision considers children's safety to be of paramount importance; the health and safety of all participants is central to everything within a Water School programme. This means exercising good practice at all times and also using the natural wetlands and beaches in a safe and sustained way. This well-planned and thoughtful operation benefits future generations and is productive in educating our children about the unique qualities and characteristics of habitats in their natural environment. Operating a provision with strict health and safety rules ensures the safety of the children, adults, and nature itself. The aim is to make children, parents, and staff aware of health and safety issues and to minimise the hazards and risks, so enabling the children to thrive.

Water School leaders must be fully trained in risk assessment and emergency outdoor first aid as they must implement a health and safety policy, risk assess the sites seasonally and daily, and risk assess activities and tools. Adult helpers also need sufficient, specific training, especially when the activities the children may participate in are 'higher-risk' activities (such as campfire cooking or tool use). These activities should not be available to the children until certain behaviours and boundaries are established. Children should be encouraged and supported in recognising and managing risk for themselves, through real-life situations and experiences.

Basic health and safety rules

The following action plan provides an overview of the day-to-day running of the Water School programme as an essential reference for the educators and parents, detailing the regular events and organisational requirements:

1 Parents' permission must be obtained before the sessions.
2 Emergency contact details and medical information need to be taken to every session.

3 A 1:3 adult–child ratio needs to be provided when visiting sites away from Water School.

4 Children names must be entered daily in a register.

5 A basic first-aid kit needs to be kept for the treatment of minor injuries by qualified staff.

6 A record of all incidents must be kept.

7 A mobile telephone must be carried at all times.

8 All staff members must hold a current, appropriate first-aid certificate. The, required first-aid qualification includes first-aid training for the safety of infants and young children.

9 The first-aid kit must comply with the relevant health and safety regulations and needs to be regularly checked by a designated member of staff and re-stocked as necessary. Use of hypoallergenic plasters is required if the need arises.

10 Parents who are aware of an allergy should advise when completing their child's registration form, which also gives parents' written permission for emergency medical treatment to be given. Parents must sign and date their written approvals. Any injury requiring general practitioner or hospital treatment to be given to a child, parent, volunteer, or visitor must be reported to the owner company's Health and Safety Executive (staff members need to understand the first-aid procedures for HIV and AIDS, the disposal of sanitary waste, and uphold hygiene regulations accordingly. Protective equipment will be used by staff when dealing with spills of bodily fluids).

11 Site and equipment must be regularly checked for damage or hazards and dealt with accordingly and immediately.

12 Basic hygiene must be taught to children: hand washing, covering mouths when sneezing/coughing, using paper towels, disposing of tissues etc.

13 Only persons who have been checked by an enhanced disclosure from the Criminal Records Bureau and are registered with the relevant professional body can have unsupervised access to children, including helping them when they need the toilet. This is dealt with in an appropriate manner.

14 All tools must be regularly checked for cleanliness and safety and any dangerous items must be repaired or discarded.

15 All imported materials must be non-toxic.

16 Play needs to be constantly supervised.

17 Children need to have planned, structured training to handle and store tools safely.

18 Children need to learn about health, safety, and personal hygiene through the activities we provide and the routines we follow.

19 In the event of extreme windy weather, or if the site is not deemed safe, then cancellation may be necessary. If this is the case, the Water School leader needs to contact the parents immediately and an alternative activity must be available in such an event.

20 Children should be dressed appropriately for changeable weather. This includes footwear and headwear. If a child is not suitably dressed they will not be able to attend that session. This means: Winter 'W's (warm clothes, wellies, woolly hat, and waterproofs with trousers) and Summer 'S's (sunscreen, sunhat, NO sandals, insect spray).

21 When visiting sites away from Water School, to avoid site degradation and danger, the site must be left as it was found; the children need to be taught this principle.
22 When visiting sites away from Water School, any disturbance must be notified to the landowner or local authority.

Tools, resources, and equipment

The children will be provided with resources and equipment to help them visualise and extend their knowledge, skills, interests, and aptitudes; these also help to promote continuity and progression. A sufficient quantity and quality of equipment and resources need to be provided for the number of children attending. We provide sufficient challenge and meet the needs and interests of all children through natural and recycled materials that are in good condition and safe for the children to use. Equipment needs to be checked regularly and review dates must be recorded. Unsafe, worn-out, dirty, or damaged equipment needs to be repaired and cleaned, or replaced if necessary. The provision of activities and appropriate resources must be carefully planned to give an appropriate balance of familiar equipment and resources as well as offering new and exciting challenges.

Organising trips away from Water School

Before the day

Inform each party about their responsibilities on the trip, including: who writes the risk assessments and therefore is responsible for health and safety; who collects the consent and medical information; who is in charge of discipline; what activities are planned; where responsibilities begin and end.

Always provide two copies of the following:

- risk assessments
- contact sheets
- consent forms
- normal operating procedure
- emergency operating procedure.

Place one set in the Water School file held within the school and give one to the group leader.

Equipment

First-aid kit, bin bags, a copy of the consent forms, mobile phone, fresh drinking water, sun cream, spare warm tops, spare waterproofs, all individual information and medication for participants, a dry bag containing all medical and consent forms, specific equipment for activities, snack (possibly warm drink in cold weather), tarpaulin, string, rope, knife or scissors.

Before leaving

- Hold a briefing meeting with the other partners and adults on the trip so that everyone is aware of the policies and the timetable of the day.
- A quick briefing about the day with the young people, any immediate safety issues in relation to transport, and what sort of behaviour is expected from the group and individuals. Explain the consequences of non-compliance. Include this in the risk assessments.
- All young people should be counted regularly and given a 'Buddy' to look after.

The visit

Statistically travel can be the most dangerous part of the trip. If there is a road accident, always call the police and follow the emergency procedure. Always have a 'second in command' if the leader needs to leave the group or anything happens to the leader, and make sure they are fully briefed in what to do in such an emergency.

Always ensure the group is briefed before they start running around, and point out the space that they are permitted to play/work in. If possible, at each session run through a basic risk assessment pointing out immediate dangers with the children and talking about the tasks expected of them. Always insist on a no litter policy.

Encourage the group of young people to count themselves regularly. At the beginning, outline the session and establish points of contact throughout the activity. Always make sure the group evaluates the trip together. With the children, count the group before leaving the site and ensure they have everything they arrived with (check what else they may have).

Emergency procedure

Accidents: ensure that other people understand that you (the leader) are responsible for the groups' safety and well-being and you are the decision maker. Deal with any first aid and minor problems with minimum fuss and record them in the accident book. If you need to call any assistance from outside the party please follow the instructions given by the emergency services personnel.

Procedure in the event of a serious incident

- Secure the group members and keep them together in a safe area; make sure everyone is safe and comfortable.
- Assess the incident and prioritise actions/injuries. Don't be afraid to seek assistance.
- Ascertain the grid reference or postcode of the location to advise the emergency services or other personnel, if they are needed. Prepare the casualty's permission form.
- Inform appropriate authorities, police, nursery office, and line manager and explain the situation. Decide who will contact the parents and keep them informed.

- Keep any casualties comfortable and warm while waiting.
- DO NOT SPEAK TO THE MEDIA. Subsequent dealings with parents and the press should be done after consulting the head teacher of the school/setting and your line manager.

Special circumstances and conditions

Children learn and develop best when they are safe, happy, and healthy. Safeguarding children is everyone's responsibility around them and must be their first and foremost consideration, therefore it is important to know how and when to raise any concerns in the Water School environment, being aware of the warning signs and alert to acting on any concerns. Being prepared and taking all possibilities into consideration will equip practitioners with the essentials to support good practice.

Child protection

As in any form of childhood education, child protection issues are paramount. Leaders need to ensure that risk assessments cover the obvious eventualities and that they instruct staff members to remain vigilant at all times and be aware of new risks if they arise. Children need to work in groups of two or three, and are never intentionally left alone. Non-qualified staff members must be supported at all times and never left alone with young people.

Lost child procedures

In the event of a child becoming lost while at Water School, the leader needs to apply appropriate practice procedures. These ensure a systematic approach to find the lost child with consideration given to the levels of risk to the child. In the event that a child is lost, the leader must ensure a search is made for the child as soon as possible, parents and authorities are notified at the appropriate stage, and a high level of care is maintained for the other children in the group while procedures are followed. The leader must check the register to confirm the child attended Water School. A quick search of surrounding areas can take place by an appointed adult. While the initial search is being made, the session supervisor should make enquiries of all adults to establish details of the last sighting of the child: time, clothes that the child was wearing, and the mental state of the child (happy, upset etc.). The supervisor should then telephone the police, report the situation, follow their advice, and contact the parent or carer. Telephone lines should remain as free as possible so that messages are not delayed. The activities for the remaining children must continue as normally as possible and staff not involved in the search must give the children their full attention.

Weather conditions

Poor weather and shelter

Water School sessions should ideally be organised in all weather conditions; exposure to the elements is part of the magic of nature and therefore an integral part of Water School; however there are a few exceptions:

1   strong winds that make woodland areas hazardous for use due to falling debris;
2   when it is dangerous to get to the site by road, for example due to snow or ice;
3   very wet and cold conditions, where hypothermia is a real possibility.

In inclement and/or cold weather, the Water School leaders must be able to erect temporary shelters to enable the participants to take shelter at required times. These shelters consist of large or small tarpaulins and suitable rope for securing them. This equipment must form part of the general Water School kit. Shelters can be erected quickly and easily in a manner appropriate to the layout and orientation of the Water School site being used. If there is a suitable site and sufficient raw materials available, a more permanent shelter can be constructed. Ground tarpaulins must be taken to provide comfort in cooler months. In the summer, natural features can provide good sun cover but shelters made from tarpaulins should be built if required.

Seasons and their effects on the site

As beach profiles transform due to the changes in seasons and natural energy, Water School sites vary from large, open spaces to narrow, sandy paths. The beach profile results from natural elements forcing changes during the seasonal cycle. Many beaches are affected by storms, waves, and wind, forming summer beaches and winter beaches in all natural wetlands. Summer beaches can be smoother and wider, while winter beaches tend to be narrower, and can, for example, have little berm and offshore sand bars.

Summer conditions move sand onto the beach, while winter storm waves move sand offshore. Unusually large storm events result in a disequilibrium profile, and sand may be permanently lost to deep water. Summer and winter beach profiles are expressions of the seasonal cycle of wave energy. Due to storms, waves are larger and more energetic in winter than in summer.

Temperature and wind

Wind can be dangerous as much as it can be fun. First and foremost, young children must be dressed in layers and proper outdoor wear. As young children are typically unable to communicate if they are cold, the adults must assess the weather conditions and check the children regularly. If they feel cold to the touch (feel their head or hands) or seem lethargic, they are cold and should be brought indoors immediately. Keep outdoor playtime short. Go outdoors twice a day for 20 to 30 minutes each time, rather than once a day for an hour or longer.

In winter, hats and mittens should be worn by young children whenever going outdoors, even if just for a few minutes, and spare items must be carried during all outdoor sessions. Water-resistant outerwear and footwear is the best option, because clothing that can get wet will cause children to get colder much more quickly, significantly increasing the risk of frostbite.

In general terms, cold weather can be categorised as the following:

1   chilly and generally uncomfortable
2   cold
3   very cold

4   bitterly cold with significant risk of frostbite
5   extreme cold and frostbite is likely
6   frigid and exposed skin will freeze in 1 minute.

Day care facilities and preschools should have strict policies designating a minimum outdoor temperature for children to be able to play outdoors. If you follow the above temperature guidelines keep in mind that there is more to the science than just temperature. Wind chill factors and proper attire are part of the equation. National weather services all over the world provide helpful wind chill charts, giving approximate times for frostbite on exposed skin to set in, and although the charts are usually based on testing adults, not children, they are an excellent starting point for being cautious with children.

Other environmental factors

Tide safety

Natural elements – such as tides and floods – have a considerable effect on certain Water School sites and the activities that can be carried out. In the Water School programme, the sites should be entered at different times to demonstrate the changes in nature to the children and to engage them in different activities. It is important to remember that calm waters can quickly turn into violent waves or currents that can easily sweep people away. It is advised to check and note the tide times prior to each visit. Groups should always indicate their expected time of return.

DIFFERENT TYPES OF TIDES

Tides are the periodic rise and fall of large bodies of water. Winds and currents move the surface water causing waves. The gravitational attraction of the moon causes the seas and oceans to bulge out in the direction of the moon; these are called lunar tides. Another move occurs on the opposite side of the Earth, since the Earth is also being pulled toward the moon and away from the water on the far side. Ocean levels fluctuate daily as the sun, the moon, and the Earth interact physically. As the moon travels around the Earth and as they travel around the sun together, the combined gravitational forces cause the world's waters to rise and fall. Since the Earth is rotating while this is happening, two tides occur each day. Lunar tides are created because the Earth and the moon are attracted to each other, like magnets. The moon has a magnetic attraction and pulls at anything on the Earth to bring it closer, but the Earth is able to hold on to everything except the water, therefore the moon is able to pull at it and it is always moving. Each day, there are two high tides and two low tides. The ocean is constantly moving from high tide to low tide and then back to high tide and so on. There is roughly a 12 hours 25 minutes-long period between two high tides.

When the sun and moon are aligned, there are exceptionally strong gravitational forces, causing very high and very low tides, called spring tides. Spring tides are especially strong as the gravitational forces of the moon and the sun both contribute to them. Spring tides occur during the full moon and the new moon. When the sun and moon are not aligned, the gravitational forces cancel each other out, and the tides are not as dramatically high or low; these are called neap tides. Neap tides are especially weak tides; they occur when the gravitational forces of the moon and the sun are perpendicular to one another (with respect to the Earth) during quarter moons.

The proxigean spring tide is a rare, unusually high tide. This very high tide occurs when the moon is both unusually close to the Earth (at its closest perigee, called the proxigee) and in the new moon phase (when the moon is between the sun and the Earth). The proxigean spring tide occurs, at most, once every 1.5 years.

Rip currents

A rip current, commonly referred to simply as a rip, or rip tide, is a strong channel of water flowing seaward from near the shore, typically through the surf line. Typical flow is at 0.5 metres per second and can be as fast as 2.5 metres per second. They can move to different locations on a beach break, up to tens of metres (a few hundred feet) a day. They can occur at any beach with breaking waves, including oceans, seas, and large lakes. When wind and waves push water toward the shore, that water is often forced sideways by the oncoming waves. This water streams along the shoreline until it finds an exit back to the open water. The resulting rip current is usually narrow and located in a trench between sandbars or under piers. A common misconception is that ordinary undertow or even rip currents are strong enough to pull someone under the surface of the water but in reality the current is strongest at the surface. This strong surface flow tends to dampen incoming waves, leading to the illusion of a particularly calm part of the water, which may possibly lure some swimmers into the area. Rip currents are stronger when the surf is rough, for example during high onshore winds or when the tide is low.

Rip currents are a source of danger for people in ocean and lake surf, dragging swimmers away from the beach. Death by drowning follows exhaustion while fighting the river or ocean current. It is important for Water School leaders to know that, although a rare event, rip currents can be deadly for non-swimmers as well, because a person standing waist deep in water can be dragged into deeper waters, where they can drown if they are unable to swim and are not wearing an appropriate flotation device. Varying topography makes some beaches more likely to have rip currents, so it is sensible to check prior to choosing a Water School location.

A swimmer caught in a rip current should not attempt to swim back to shore directly against the rip, as they risk exhaustion and drowning. A rip does not pull a swimmer under water; it carries the swimmer away from the shore in a narrow channel of water. The swimmer should remain calm and swim parallel to the shore until out of the current – like stepping off a treadmill – then try to float back toward the shore. A swimmer who is unable to swim away from a strong rip, should relax and calmly float or tread water to conserve energy, raise one hand, and shout for help. Eventually the rip will lose strength, and the swimmer can swim at a leisurely pace in a diagonal direction, away from the rip, back to shore. Water School leaders should understand the danger of rip currents, learn how to recognise them and how to escape from them, and only swim in areas where lifeguards are operating, whenever possible.

RIP CURRENT EMERGENCY PLAN

1   stay calm – don't panic;
2   if you can stand, wade; do not swim;
3   keep hold of your board or inflatable to help you float;
4   raise your hand and shout for help;
5   never try to swim directly against the rip or you will get exhausted;
6   try to swim parallel to the beach until free of the rip, then make for shore;
7   if you see someone else in trouble, call 999 or 112 and ask for the coastguard.

A unique approach to health and safety: taking acceptable risks based on believing in children

> The biggest 'risk' in the environment of young children is when there is no risk, because this unavoidably leads to risk averse, inexperienced and unconfident young children.
>
> (Horvath, 2010)

Health and safety is always something that will come into the limelight of education as children's safety is its most important factor. However, all health and safety implications should be considered with regard to children's welfare, including the benefits of allowing children to take acceptable risks by making their own choices. One of the most serious risks of education is protecting children from encountering any real-life opportunities; preventing children from naturally challenging themselves will adversely affect their development. Contemporary research (Sandseter, 2007; Little and Dawber, 2008) shows that risk-taking contributes to the personal development of young children, and by not allowing them to take risks their development is negatively transformed.

Early years curriculums all over the world represent a common vision that every child is a unique, confident, and competent part of the community, and the practitioners need to find the best possible ways of supporting the children to grow into this role. Children learn from adults, from other children, and from the environment around them. Believing in this is a collective, crucial base of all pedagogies that realise our image of the unique child as a resourceful individual, in whose abilities adults need to have confidence, teaching through taking the responsibility for communicating what things, how and why they are being done. The beliefs, knowledge, and methods of educators create the pedagogical base, making the learning visible as the joint effort of all co-constructors: the children, the educators, the parents, society, and other cultures. This level of understanding the context in which the educators' unique pedagogical questions arise, while respecting the local social and cultural traditions, creates trust. The principles of the curriculum set out that the educators' main duty is to gain an understanding of how each child learns and grows confident and competent. The learning curve is thus led by the child's initiative and based on the view of each unique child, trusting their ability to make the right choices. This attitude leads to a relaxed approach to health and safety that considers the risks of activities in light of their benefits.

In the Water School approach the understanding of the changing nature of the situation, the children, and the environment is critical. This leads to risk assessments that consider the resources and tools and contain a collection of experiences, rather than describing possible outcomes of activities, and therefore provide a base knowledge that the educators can draw upon in different situations. It results in lively, responsive, and energetic behaviour from educators, acknowledging that it is impossible to prepare for every possibility and to assess all risks in advance.

Therefore, in Water School there are two types of risk assessments:

1   *Responsive risk aware behaviour*: responsive risk management is about using observations and reflecting in the actual situations, considering the benefits proportional to the risk, finding and encouraging children's interests, exploring whether as practitioners we are comfortable with the situation, deciding if we shall intervene or whether it is possible to carry on safely (which ultimately leads to the formation of unique and new teaching methods). See p.100.
2   *Resource risk assessment*: a collection of experiences describing what practitioners need to be aware of when using certain resources in various activities. See p.101.

The concept of risk awareness and real-time assessment provides a balanced view of risky play. While the authoritative, practical document will assist educators in weighing up the risks against the benefits, they will also develop a positive attitude with an ever up-to-date and valid view of situations, with the individual child's needs as the focus.

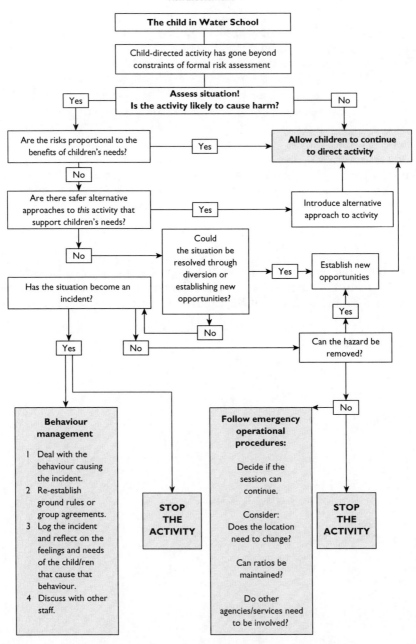

**Water School
situation-based responsive
risk assessment**

The child in Water School

Child-directed activity has gone beyond
constraints of formal risk assessment

**Assess situation!
Is the activity likely to cause harm?**

Yes

No

Are the risks proportional to the
benefits of children's needs?

Yes

No

**Allow children to continue
to direct activity**

Are there safer alternative
approaches to *this* activity that
support children's needs?

Yes

Introduce alternative
approach to activity

No

Could
the situation be
resolved through
diversion or
establishing new
opportunities?

Yes

Establish new
opportunities

Has the situation become an
incident?

No

Yes

Yes

Yes

No

Can the hazard be
removed?

No

**Behaviour
management**

1 Deal with the
   behaviour causing
   the incident.
2 Re-establish
   ground rules or
   group agreements.
3 Log the incident
   and reflect on the
   feelings and needs
   of the child/ren
   that cause that
   behaviour.
4 Discuss with other
   staff.

**STOP
THE
ACTIVITY**

**Follow emergency
operational
procedures:**

Decide if the
session can
continue.

Consider:
Does the location
need to change?

Can ratios be
maintained?

Do other
agencies/services need
to be involved?

**STOP
THE
ACTIVITY**

Resource risk assessment

Date of assessment: 05 December 2014   Assessor: *Judit Horvath*

Resource/tool: **Knife**

Possible uses: Used by adults/children in activities

Possible use *What do you do with it?*	Hazard *What harm can it cause?*	People at risk *Who can get hurt?*	Existing control measures *What do you do to avoid harm?*	Benefits of Activity *Why is it good?*
Storing	Accessible to children, becoming unsuitable for use due to poor condition e.g. rusty	Children and adults	Tool to be kept in allocated secure place at all times when not in use All staff first-aid trained and competent	Raising confidence Growing self-esteem and self-respect Better self-care Ability to understand cause and effect Develops fine-motor skills Develops listening skills Joy and achievement
Carrying	Hitting, throwing Slips, trips and falls Standing on	Children and adults	Children to be educated how to carry tools Maintain ratios all the time. Establishing rules for safe carrying All staff first-aid trained and competent If the knife is dropped to be picked up immediately Ensure is knife kept out of walkways, good housekeeping	
Using in activities by adults	Injury due to piercing or cutting	Children and adults	Tools checked regularly to ensure no broken parts Children to work with secure, sufficient distance from each other Always use safety gloves on non-working hand Staff to supervise children at all times Maintain ratio. All staff first-aid trained and competent	
Using in activities by children	Inappropriate use Injury due to piercing or cutting	Children and adults		
Cleaning	Injury due to piercing or cutting	Children and adults	Tools checked regularly to ensure no broken parts. Staff to supervise children at all times. Maintain ratio. All Staff trained and competent	

Changes, if any required: *Purchased new cleaning solution since last assessment*

(Seasonal) Activity ideas: *Making natural herb salad*

Chapter 6

The Water School leader in training

Introduction

In the absence of specific Water School leader training, this chapter will assist practitioners in finding suitable training to support them in delivering the programme. It will point out the possibilities that the existing outdoor educator training programmes and alternative forms of training (such as networking, in-house training) offer to those planning to deliver Water School sessions.

The educational possibilities with Water Schools are endless. The philosophy and ethos can be adapted to many different sites, many different educational settings, and in many different ways. All Water Schools must be led by qualified leaders who are qualified educators – not necessarily Water School leaders, as there is no specific training for this. Forest School and Beach School leader qualifications take about a year to obtain and involve delivering practice sessions and demonstrating knowledge through the completion of a workbook. Training with an accredited Beach School training provider will equip interested educators with all the knowledge, skills, and confidence they need to run effective and safe Water School sessions for a target group. Applicants need to be qualified to work with children and have a passion for – or experience of – outdoor play and learning. The training providers, however, state clearly that trainees can be working with children from a range of settings and focusing on a variety of ages. The practical activities on the courses enable participants to understand the development of Water Schools, apply it directly to a chosen group and be able to identify and use case studies in the use of wetlands as an educational resource from an international and local perspective.

The starting point

Given that Water School is a brand new concept, there is no particular training that prepares a qualified Water School leader. However, when looking for Water School related training, a number of different providers can be found offering Beach School leader courses. The number of Beach School leader training opportunities can seem overwhelming; there are also different ways in which the qualification can be achieved. Each provider is different and therefore the standards of training and understanding outdoor approaches can differ greatly. Some of the trainers have been delivering outdoor practitioner training courses for over a decade and they may be members of the relevant trainers' networks locally or internationally. High-quality training is really important and providers who offer reflective practice and ongoing development are the best choices. While different kinds of outdoor education can be found in Australia, New Zealand, Malaysia, and Germany, with practitioners from China, Japan, Italy, France, Norway, Sweden, Ireland, and many more, travelling from all over the world, accredited Water School training is still relatively rare.

There are various levels of training available with different course contents, and while interested people can choose appropriate training for them, once a course is completed – according to the leader training provider, Archimedes Training Ltd (n.d.) – all learners aiming to deliver outdoor sessions for children should be able to:

1 understand the sustainable way to set up a Water School learning environment;
2 manage the water/beach ecosystems as a learning resource through the development of understanding of the ecological structure;
3 develop an understanding of the ecological structure;
4 manage methods of local natural water ecosystems;
5 demonstrate how to use and teach a range of practical skills appropriate to Water Schools to include: temporary shelters using appropriate knots and resources, fire lighting and beach cooking fires;
6 use various pedagogical approaches to designing and delivering Water School sessions;
7 apply effective reflective processes;
8 assist children in the development of emotional intelligence and social skills;
9 understand the unique health and safety requirements for running Water Schools, including tidal forecasts, seasons and tides, fires, and landowners;
10 carry out benefits analyses and support the safety of their group;
11 adapt to basic good working practice procedures.

Good Beach School leader training should qualify people who can be utilised independently to assure practitioners – and those employing them – that children's safety is paramount and that the use of the marine shores and beaches can be sustained for future generations, as well as being productive in educating using their unique qualities and habitats (Archimedes Training, n.d.).

Beach School training can be a suitable professional development for teachers, youth workers, play workers, and rangers alike, as it offers the optimum combination of practical and tool skills, land and ecological management, leadership and risk evaluation, and the application of learning theory.

Training needs to be planned ahead before an establishment sets up a Water School provision. It is worth considering the time frame needed to apply and plan who is best placed to be involved in this process. Many settings may find that approaching training from a team perspective is particularly useful, a typical method is to have one fully trained leader working with one or two internally trained assistants. Not all of the staff working at Water School need to be externally qualified, as simply being committed makes the preparation and delivery of Water School successful. During the training, outdoor spaces within the setting can be a good starting point to deliver sessions; however getting children off-site into a designated Water School site is the best option.

Networking

In order to maintain high standards of Water School provision, it is important to be an active member of a thematic network that aims and works to set common standards (of pedagogy, policy, and procedures) and share best practice.

Leader/educator networking usually brings unprecedented opportunities into education and the modern tools enable teachers to collaborate, share, and discuss ideas with other teachers, almost instantly.

Being out of the classroom with children can be an extremely isolated position and the exploration of innovative pedagogies can become very difficult. Professional development networks can save time with immediate solutions, and provocations have a high impact on teachers' professional development. The power of networking has two key elements: it feeds from current, real-time practice and its method of informal professional dialogue puts the existing knowledge of educators into a different perspective. Networking operates both as leading and support/mentoring and throughout networking, educators often access new research-based teaching practices and resources. Networking is a continuous professional development opportunity that has the potential to become easily tailored to the diversity and complexity of needs that are acutely apparent in outdoor teaching.

Professional educators need constant updating of existing skills and learning of new skills, and given the modernity and young nature of Water School provision, networking can assure the sustainable future of Water School education by developing and forming the practice and pedagogy.

In the modern world, children's knowledge, interests, and therefore educational needs, are changing and adapting all the time. Education, with its framework and professionals, needs to change and adapt as well, responding to the rapidly, and often drastically, changing environment, that is the world we live in.

In-house training

In-house training courses, delivered by trained members of staff in a setting, offer a unique type of continuous development, at a time and place to suit a setting and its team.

While it does not provide qualification, it offers a wide range of benefits:

- flexibility
- time
- free learning
- tailored approach
- hands-on ideas
- teambuilding
- personal involvement and enthusiasm
- personal reward
- reflective practice
- full use of potential and expertise.

It can be difficult to release staff members to attend training, so deliver programmes at a suitable time – including evenings and weekends, at a location of the setting's choice – and this difficulty may be overcome.

Chapter 7

International examples of education through natural water

Introduction

This chapter will illustrate how different cultures appreciate natural water's educational value in various ways. It will show some contemporary educational methods that use natural water as a resource in different countries and, considering the individuality of these approaches in relation to Water School, it will determine the place of Water School in the context of other thoughts and ideas about outdoor learning.

Different educational settings all over the world value nature and natural water in many different ways. Their approaches create important links to the Water School approach and also support its theoretical framework.

Italy

The Reggio Emilia approach: garden and outdoor spaces created for nature

The Reggio Emilia approach has its origins in Italy, in the province of Reggio Emilia. Its beginnings came in the wake of Italy's post-Second World War freedom from fascist rule. The theorist behind the approach was a middle-school teacher, Loris Malaguzzi, who consulted and worked together with families to create a new system of education for young children, one that was child-centred, recognising and honouring the individuality of each child. The first Reggio Emilia schools were the results of a true community effort, being built by the families who were part of those communities. Due to the hard work of Malaguzzi, by 1963 the city government had begun to assume responsibility for the management of the people's schools and the first municipal preschool was opened.

The environment is the third teacher: utilising water in outdoor spaces

In the Reggio approach, the environment is taking centre stage and is used carefully (being mindful of how fragile it is) as a teaching setting for its potential to naturally inspire children. In a natural environment that is filled with order, light, beauty, and open spaces, every material has its natural purpose; every little space encourages and motivates children to follow their own interests, explore their ideas, and discover their own impact on the environment. The natural space accommodates children as capable individuals via its natural characteristics, given that its offerings are not age-specific or skill-limited, and the space is cared for by the children and the adults. Teachers in Reggio-inspired schools all over the world do not follow a pre-determined curriculum, but instead support the exploration and learning of the children in their care through their natural environment.

The multi-age classrooms of Reggio-inspired schools generally have two teachers, who collaborate with no hierarchy between them to help the children in their learning: researching, observing, and documenting the different stages of the work taking place. The principle of environment as the third teacher is applied readily outdoors by placing value on nature's characteristics (aesthetics, organisation, thoughtfulness, provocation, communication, and interaction). When coming into contact with natural resources – such as water – in their natural places – such as a beach – both resource and its source are treated with great respect.

The care and attention we pay to organising the space outdoors naturally stimulates children's imagination, creativity, exploration, discovery, engagement, and sense of awe. The emphasis on nature is also shown in the elements of nature being brought into the classrooms and art centres – from leaves, stones, and pebbles to rocks, branches, and sticks. An effort is also made to go outdoors into the natural environment every day, regardless of the weather.

The speciality of this approach in relation to Water School: the relationship between indoors and outdoors

The flow of energy is a strong element of the approach. The relationship between the indoor and outdoor environment influences the education and the rhythm of the indoor space directly linking to the outdoor space. A transparency must be created when a learning environment is planned with the possibility of looking through from one space to the other. This creates a unique sense of the depth of field and stimulates a different perception of spaces. In the Reggio approach children are encouraged to think and investigate in more dimensions through exploring materials and media. Few children can resist water's attraction and fascination; exploration and stimulus are key, therefore water features are often part of both the indoor and outdoor spaces.

Penn Green Children's Centre, United Kingdom: the Beach and intricate indoor waterways

Similarly to the Reggio Emilia model, Penn Green Children's Centre in Corby, UK was created in 1983, jointly funded by the local authority social services and education departments. It is a designated and integrated children's centre, which places a great emphasis on its relationship with parents. With reference to 'narrowing the gap' (National Foundation for Educational Research, 2007) and knowing that parental involvement is the key factor in allowing children to thrive, there is a strong focus on the children. In their 'Making Children's Learning Visible' programme (C4EO, n.d.), family workers judge children to be 'emerging', 'developing' or 'confident' against the development matters statements (The British Association for Early Childhood Education, n.d.) in a particular age band (irrespective of their chronological age), in each aspect of each area of learning in the early years curriculum. This is done three times during the year. These judgements are made with parents, and corresponding graphs are produced to show the progress made by individual children; these are then shared with parents.

The speciality of this approach in relation to Water School: the strong link between home learning and nursery education makes learning sustainable

Penn Green has created a welcoming environment for the whole community that nurtures the children, rather than just for the children. It is open and friendly, therefore provides a hands-on training for parents about how to share experiences with the children. The Beach is a large, outdoor sandpit in the middle of Penn Green Centre, with sails to provide shade; it has a wide range of resources for use when exploring the sandy beach experience, and a pirate ship for role play. It is surrounded by decking and window seats, and is a place for parents to be with their children. The water therapy room is where children explore water in different ways. It consists of a non-slip floor, low splash pool, a selection of showers and taps, a long, low-level sink, and an umbrella shower with lights; it is open for all different groups to use. Penn Green has also built a very large waterway system that demonstrates links between spaces and also recycles the water the children play with.

Hungary

Waldorf Nursery – Nagykanizsa (Waldorf Családi Napközi) – visiting the local park

> The essential task of the kindergarten teacher is to create the proper physical environment around the children. 'Physical environment' must be understood in the widest sense imaginable. It includes not just what happens around the children in the material sense, but everything that occurs in their environment, everything that can be perceived by their senses, that can work on the inner powers of the children from the surrounding physical space.
>
> (Steiner, 1965)

Waldorf Schools – also called Steiner Schools – are based on the educational philosophy of Rudolf Steiner, an Austrian philosopher whose educational approach connected to his spiritual philosophy. The first Waldorf School was started in Germany in 1919, following the publishing of Steiner's first book on education in 1907, *The Education of the Child* (1965). Having started as a corporate nursery for a local factory, the first school quickly grew to include a large number of students who had no connection to the factory; before long, the model had inspired the opening of similar schools around Europe. By 1938 the movement had made its way to the United States as well.

Waldorf education sees the child as a whole being, made up of body, soul, and spirit, and attempts to nurture the whole child, helping him or her to rise to their fullest potential. Waldorf Schools provide a beautiful, simple, learning environment that feels much like a home. In early childhood it is furnished with open-ended resources and activities that allow children to use their own creativity and imagination. The curriculum in a Waldorf School is not purely academic in nature, but includes art, practical activities, and physical education. Seasonal celebrations have an important role in the rhythm of life in a Waldorf School. The development of the academic curriculum is referred to as 'spiralling up' as it appeals to the natural interests of the child, based on developmental stages as they grow, and later goes 'out', taking a more in-depth look at things that have been studied in the past. In early childhood, when children learn by imitating adults, the educators act as role models; however as children grow older and seek an authority to learn from, the teacher's role will change and evolve. In an ideal situation, the same teacher will stay with a group of students throughout the eight years of elementary and middle school. This gives the teacher a unique ability to gain knowledge of the individual children, which allows for a deep level of understanding, and a close working relationship with parents, as the teacher becomes almost like another member of the child's family.

In the Waldorf *Családi Napközi* in Hungary early learning is closely connected to children's physical and sensory experience, meaning a strong belief that everything young children see, hear, or touch can have an effect on their development. During their regular visits to the local park, the clean, orderly, beautiful, and quiet environment of nature provides varied and nourishing opportunities for child-led education where children experience touch, lively and joyful movement, and a deep level of listening. The children can choose suitable experiences: large group, small group, or solitary activities – nature accommodates all. By taking children into nature and visiting the local park pond, diverse elements are integrated into the children's education, which provide surroundings accessible to all the children's understanding and feelings. The children unconsciously experience the immediate environment and gain a sense of belonging and security in the world.

The speciality of this approach in relation to Water School: using nature for what it is

According to Steiner, the natural world is infused by the spiritual world; indeed, all of physical reality is just a condensation of spiritual reality. In this sense, nature deserves our respect, even reverence. Moreover, with the Crucifixion, Christ's blood — his essence, as it were — flowed into the earth so, Steiner taught, the natural realm on Earth has a sort of holiness, and for this reason he often advocated 'green' beliefs, that – today – promote conservation, organic gardening, and ecological sensitivity. One of the educational manifestations of Steiner's philosophy is the nature table, also known as a seasonal table, which is a place indoors where children can follow the natural cycle of the year. The nature table ensures that all the changes that are taking place in the natural world can be expressed. The objects and materials on the table follow, and visually represent, the essence of what is happening in nature, so creating and maintaining a nature table supports observation of the learning procedure. The idea is based on the theory that young children are unconsciously aware of nature and its laws.

Balaton Camp Beach and Forest School, Balatonakali: utilising Lake Balaton

There are a number of educational institutes in Hungary that use natural water (local lakes and rivers) as a teaching resource regularly in their annual curriculum and as summer courses. Lake Balaton, a very popular natural destination, is situated in the middle of the country and has several Water Schools. Balatonakali is one of the most popular places on the northern shore of Lake Balaton. The summer Water School can be found 400 metres north of the city centre in Balaton National Park. It aims to operate as a teaching hub for local schools, providing an organised programme to learn through play and to widen children's knowledge about the history of the water world, and about the local environment and its heritage. It teaches children about the biological and social importance of Lake Balaton. There are specific programmes to cater for different interests such as, map reading and navigation around Balaton, natural obstacle courses, the management and protection of Lake Balaton, local flora and fauna, and nature photography. There are trained leaders of these programmes, and schools can request local rangers to guide them. There are one-day programmes where the children learn basic safety rules and get a deeper understanding of a specific area through the activities. They also offer one-week programmes for a complete nature experience and long-term learning benefits for children of all ages.

The speciality of this approach in relation to Water School: ensuring sustainability and heritage

Lake Balaton has a fascinating history, due to its important location in the centre of the country. History is being introduced through modern historical interpretation and enquiry, to raise young children's understanding of time and heritage through telling stories, demonstrating old customs, and through the historical markers of biology.

United Kingdom

Local childminder network: utilising the beach and the sea

Local educators, who have grown up in a coastal town or city, naturally use the beach as an educational resource, providing learning activities about the beach environment – the sea, the nature and uses of beaches, sand dunes, dune animals and vegetation, the impact of humans on the beach, beach and sea protection, and the surrounding areas. Their beach education covers a wide range of curriculum areas with an emphasis on social development and environmental knowledge, to develop the abilities of the children, their families, and their community to use the beach in a sustainable way.

There are many opportunities for childminders to use the Southend-on-Sea (Essex) beach site, to enhance their local programme and also to give real dimension to related topics. The education programme includes a teacher-led site visit and occasionally a guided site visit. Topics include science, geography, and history, approached as a single subject and as a cross-curriculum project. The childminders' general beach visits include lots of play but also provide opportunities to explore basics of science, coastal geography, and history. The aim of adult-led sessions and field trip sessions is to provide the children with guidance to enhance the visit and to provide experiences to take away and build upon in the future.

Practical activities include exploration of the plants and the special adaptations that allow them to survive in their environment; looking at birds and invertebrates; life in the sea; and threats to the beach (local and global). Geography-focused sessions look at how the beach was formed and shaped by nature; forms of erosion; exploring sand, rocks, and pebbles; making pebble creations; connection to melt water rivers; physical forces that shape the beach through observing tidal changes; and the basic recording of environmental conditions, weather, and tides. They often observe the history of the beach by looking at old books and photos, to discover what nature does and how the beach is preserved, while at the same time attracting people to appreciate this valuable habitat. They create stories, trying to guess who uses the beach and how the community and the beach ecology connect.

The speciality of this approach in relation to Water School: freedom is the key

Their aim is to nurture individuals who will be self-motivated and happy. Using this programme the childminders offer children the opportunity to explore and express their inner nature, communicate their ideas and develop their own understanding of the world, without the educators placing adult assumptions and interpretations on the children's ideas. In this programme the beach is a place without limits on opportunities and questions; it engages children's curiosity, which is the best way for children's sense of freedom to learn. When children are truly free, surrounded by adults who do not determine exactly what childcare should look like, adults can see their real individual needs. In this programme the adults – who are flexible, self-reflective and continuously developing – provide an environment for ongoing wonder, allowing true freedom of mind and spirit.

Olympus KeyMed Day Nursery: utilising the nearby river

This programme, used by a middle-sized corporate day nursery setting, utilises the local brook (Prittle Brook), located behind the nursery premises, realising that Water School can be much more than learning at the seaside. Prittle Brook is a 'stream' brook in Essex, England. The green space, parallel to the brook, makes the pathway an enjoyable route for walking and cycling, and provides access to education and healthy exercise while enhancing the natural biodiversity of the area.

Within the brook there are small streams, small natural dams, clear water tumbling between the rocks, and tiny waterfalls, giving home to a vast array of plant and animal species to discover – very different from those at the seaside. The brook has a steep shore and often changes its height due to weather conditions, for example in heavy rain. There are clear marks on the shore that indicate how high the water rises, creating a low, middle, and upper shore. The sudden changes are a very interesting subject for the children to study, along with the vast array of plants, insects, reptiles, birds, and small mammals in the area.

Apart from its potential as a natural learning place, the brook is unfortunately littered with non-biodegradable waste which is being transported with the water-flow. Within this programme the children are taught about the species found in and around the brook, and they have opportunities to experience natural forces, such as the power of water, rain, and wind. It also helps them to learn about the sustainable management of its environment and offers opportunities for the children to participate in the nature conservation process. A typical 'Riverside School' session includes planning activities with the children, collecting resources, getting ready, carrying out a general site survey and risk assessment, activities (e.g. pond dipping, discovery, learning a new skill, identifying local species, collecting resources), and circle time: evaluation with the children and extension activities (whittling, nature art). The 'Riverside School' aims to help the owner company's environmental group to fight against local pollution by adopting healthy and helpful habits with the children.

The speciality of this approach in relation to Water School: adaptation to spaces, environmental focus

Though Prittle Brook was shaped and changed for industrial and agricultural purposes, this small waterway channel is a valuable aquatic wildlife habitat and – when given the chance – can teach the children a great deal. Different parts of the brook are colonised by plants and animals. Its slow flows and managed water levels provide a unique habitat that can become a vital resource for wildlife. The brook bank – where land and water meet – is particularly valuable for biodiversity. The structure and vegetation cover provide habitat for a wide variety of wildlife including dragonflies, water birds, squirrels, foxes, and hedgehogs. The hedgerow, along the brook, provides shelter and food for many animals. The cutting and the embankment are essential parts of Prittle Brook's structure. The habitats on its slopes include rock exposures, grassland, trees, and scrub. Some parts of it have been designated as of local significance for its urban wildlife, adding to the diversity of habitats on the waterway network. Its grassy embankment areas are particularly suitable for wild flowers, including cowslips and orchids, and there is often a rich insect fauna associated with this kind of grassland vegetation.

Scotland

Nature Kindergarten Mindstretchers: a lake in the middle of the forest

> Imagine a world where the lines were harsh and unyielding, the textures were consistent and variation is unheard of. Does it inspire you? Now imagine a place where the carpet changes every day, the ceiling is a myriad of different colours, light, shadow and movement. The feelings and movement completely surround you, sometimes breezy, sometimes cold, others warm. Unexpected wonders fly by, sometimes full of colour and sometimes full of noise and movement. If we really want children to thrive we need to let their connection to nature nurture them.
>
> (Warden, 2007)

Claire Warden's fascinating, world-famous, early years setting is a nature kindergarten that has redefined outdoor play in its own climate and culture, looking at the basic elements of nature and exploring, and stretching children's learning potential. Whistlebrae Nature Kindergarten and Auchlone Nature Kindergarten in Perth and Kinross, Scotland, UK, are outdoor nurseries that work with children from 2–6 years old, as well as offering after-school care and holiday care for children up to 12 years. Children spend up to 90 per cent of the time outdoors. The three spaces – the secure natural space indoors; the gently challenging outdoor investigative zone, which helps young children to develop emotional confidence and skills; and the wild wood, where they can feel the freedom of a fully natural environment – are designed to develop children's skills and confidence in the natural world. The environment (with all three spaces) is eco-friendly, using natural fair trade resources, organic food, and alternative energy sources.

The speciality of this approach in relation to Water School: the importance of the child-centred approach

The approach appreciates that each child is an individual, regardless of their background, and celebrates children's differing abilities, strengths, and needs. Children's work is highly valued to 'create creators', highlighting the process of creativity rather than the end product. As an environmentally friendly nursery they encourage transient art with natural materials, which are photographed to record the process. The curriculum is child and nature based, where the majority of the learning takes place outdoors; children can explore concepts and achieve the expected outcomes in a very practical, sensorial, active, and contextual manner. It achieves a higher order of thinking, problem-solving, self-risk-assessing, and complex communication by involving children in everything. The children's personal experiences and learning are recorded in the 'Talking and Thinking Floor' books, which are completed with the children.

Cowgate Under 5s Centre: the inner-city approach

This nursery provides a unique approach to children's learning in the heart of Edinburgh. The centre is run with a strong, Froebelian influence, where the belief is that, through engaging with the world, understanding unfolds. A child's natural vehicle for learning is play, a creative, expressive activity that helps children to become aware of their place in the world. Cowgate aims to provide encouraging, autonomous play in a safe environment, including elements such as a woodwork bench with real tools, believing that by allowing the children the opportunity to use real tools and materials, the understanding of safety and confidence will be developed naturally. Children are encouraged to develop independence and self-esteem. A great deal of importance is placed on the outdoors and spending time outdoors in all weathers, with an emphasis on the unity of indoors and outdoors. In this setting a greenhouse provides a unique opportunity for children to grow their own flowers, fruits, and vegetables, which can then be eaten for a snack. In this process children are encouraged to care for the environment and all the birds, insects, and other little creatures with which they share the world.

The speciality of this approach in relation to Water School:
cultivating emotional harmony through the environment

The Cowgate ethos is based on the Froebel approach. Froebel, the German educationalist, laid the foundations for modern education systems based on the recognition that children have unique needs and capabilities. Froebel advocated outdoor play provision as essential for children's learning and development. He also believed that children learn best through spontaneous child-centred play, and that they should be surrounded by kindness, understanding, and beauty. He sought to encourage the creation of educational environments that involve practical work and the direct use of natural materials. He developed a series of natural materials known as 'gifts' and a series of recommended activities or 'occupations'. Gifts were natural objects that were fixed in form; the purpose was that in playing with the object the child would learn the direct underlying concept represented by the object. This approach celebrated order in nature, and focused on nature to observe the real purpose of things. Occupations allowed more freedom and consisted of natural things that children could shape and manipulate such as clay, sand, string, and wood. There was an underlying symbolic meaning that was identified by the teachers in everything that was done, where clean-up time was seen as a reminder of nature's plan for moral and social order.

Denmark

Globussen: a forest at the seaside

In Denmark, given the natural environment of the country, outdoor areas range from vast surrounding forests to generous open spaces where children have 'space' to live outdoors and nature is considered an important vehicle in learning. There are a large number of early years and school settings that utilise the natural areas, including the forest and the surrounding beaches. Because of adequate space and time to pursue self-chosen interests and skills, children are allowed to be immersed in the natural environment, they do not become frustrated, and there is little conflict between the children themselves or between the children and adults. Children are seen to be valued throughout, they are valued as 'competent learners' and childhood is 'celebrated'. Based on this pedagogical approach, educators appreciate the times spent outdoors and, rather than understanding it as extra-curricular activity, the nature visits are built into the curriculum. In Globussen Kindergarten at Svendborg, children travel to the local seaside forest by bus, which the school also uses to transport its visitors. They have a true responsibility in getting ready, which includes three-year-olds carrying equipment from the bus to the forest gathering point, where there are designated areas for storing the equipment, making the fire, and designing the programme of the day. Throughout the period of getting ready, educators and children often stop to talk. Children are allowed to walk through the forest and onto the beach; it is obvious that they have developed a sense of belonging and safety, they understand and respect the rules and they happily communicate their personal discoveries.

The speciality of this approach in relation to Water School:
the importance of pedagogy, mixing approaches

In the Danish context children's learning is transparent and exists as the result of a complex education system, consisting of the school, the pedagogues, the family, the society, cultures, traditions, and – most importantly – the children themselves. The questions of how children learn, how to educate, and which educational concepts to follow, are firmly at the centre of focus of all early years settings. They state that, although learning from excellent practices and alternative pedagogical approaches is necessary for growth, the key factor of educational excellence is an understanding of the context in which a setting's own pedagogical questions arise. Then – respecting the surrounding social and cultural traditions – educators must find the best possible paths for the actual children in the setting. This process is based on following and understanding the individual child. The entire system supports Danish ambitions for children's development in that they enjoy safe, but attractive, challenging surroundings, that cater for their individual learning and growing needs.

Creating pedagogy this way has the potential to highlight new ways of working within the context of the political and social environment, based on individuals and those in a setting's care. This process requires educators to have new expectations of themselves, and regardless of whichever method a setting chooses to follow, educators must turn their own vision into reality and create a place (physically and mentally) where every child really matters. Many modern governments believe that every young person should experience the world beyond the traditional frame of education as an essential part of their individual learning experience and developmental process, whatever their age, abilities, or circumstances. The Danish approach supports educators to do the same: experiencing the world beyond 'just teaching' by listening, observing, and being thoughtful. Much of the educator's work can be effective only if there is an understanding of the need to observe (Learning + Teaching Scotland, 2005). Cultivating an attitude of wonder alongside the children and listening to them allows us to recognise and value learning as it occurs, as a process of change. Evaluating and redefining our own views show that education – as we know it – arises from the different experiences of all – children, families, and educators alike, and as the children, families, and educators change, so will the pedagogy.

New Zealand

'Life's a Beach': coastal education resource

'Life's a Beach' is a coastal education resource kit which provides learning activities about the beach environment. The resource covers a wide range of curriculum areas with an emphasis on science and social science. The activities contained in the resource can be used or adapted for use with different age groups. The 'Life's a Beach' resource kit has been jointly developed by Indigo Pacific and the Bay of Plenty Regional Council and was released in May 2013. 'Life's a Beach' is provided free for all education providers to use within their teaching programmes with a special focus on sustainability.

Through this programme they aim to develop: awareness and sensitivity to the environment and the diversity of the beach; knowledge and understanding of human responsibilities; attitudes and values that reflect feelings that recognise beaches as a concern for their communities; skills involved in identifying flora and fauna; and a sense of responsibility through participation and action. The programme targets the main curriculum areas, and the activities contained in it are used for levels 2 to 8 of the New Zealand school curriculum. Teaching and learning activities are saved as computer-based files and the text can be extracted and modified for education purposes only.

The speciality of this approach in relation to Water School:
Water School on a large scale, utilising the ocean
supported by modern information technology

The resource promotes a variety of natural learning strategies that are all student-centred learning approaches; the educators are seen as the facilitators of learning and children are encouraged to actively participate in their own learning. Its teaching and learning methods are adaptable to many different settings and countries. The enquiry learning involves exploration, question asking, discovering, testing and understanding of new learning, developing new skills such as observation, reasoning, critical thinking, and the ability to justify or negate existing knowledge. The action learning employs enquiry-learning strategies with an emphasis on students taking action and reflecting on the resulting changes. The cooperative learning encourages students to work together in groups, developing interpersonal skills and shared responsibility for learning. The experiential learning actively involves children in activities designed to offer an experience from which new learning can emerge. The reflection and reflective learning highlights the importance of reflection as part of the learning process in all of the other models.

Bibliography

Amabile, T. M. (1996). *Creativity in Context: Update to the Social Psychology of Creativity*. Boulder, CO: Westview Press.

Andreasen, N. C. (2011). A journey into chaos: creativity and the unconscious. In A. R. Singh and S. A. Singh (eds), *Brain, Mind and Consciousness: An International, Interdisciplinary Perspective* (pp. 42–53). Mumbai: Medknow Publications and Media.

Archimedes Training Ltd (n.d.). Available online: http://www.archimedes-training.co.uk/our-training/beach-schools/ [Accessed: 15 July 2015].

Aristotle (n.d.). *Metaphysics*. Available online: http://www.perseus.tufts.edu/hopper/text?doc =Perseus%3Atext%3A1999.01.0052%3Abook%3D1%3Asection%3D983b [Accessed: 5 July 2015].

Axline, V. (1950). Entering the child's world via play experiences. *Progressive Education*, 27, 68–75.

Bandura, A. (1971). *Psychological Modeling*. New York: Lieber-Atherton.

Bandura, A. (1977). *Social Learning Theory*. Englewood Cliffs, NJ: Prentice Hall.

Barnes, M. (2001). *An Introduction to Play Therapy*. Available online: http://www.playtherapy.org.uk/Resources/Articles/ArticleMBIntro1.htm [Accessed: 5 July 2015].

Bedford, T. A. (2004). Learning styles: a review of literature (first draft). Toowoomba, OPACS, The University of Southern Queensland.

Best Beginnings: Alaska's Early Childhood Investment (n.d.). Available online: http://www.bestbeginningsalaska.org/activities-resources/child-development-areas [Accessed: 5 July 2015].

The British Association for Early Childhood Education (n.d.). Available online: https://www.early-education.org.uk/development-matters [Accessed: 16 July 2015].

Buck, J. (1948). The H-T-P technique, a qualitative and quantitative scoring method. *Journal of Clinical Psychology*, 4(4), 317.

Buck, J. (1981). *The House-Tree-Person Technique: A Revised Manual*. Los Angeles, CA: Western Psychological Services.

C4EO (n.d.). *Families, Parents and Carers Pen Green Evidence Based Practice: Making Children's Learning Visible*. Available online: http://archive.c4eo.org.uk/themes/families/vlpdetails.aspx? lpeid=451 [Accessed: 15 July 2015].

Danks, F and Schofield, J. (2005). *Nature's Playground*. London: Frances Lincoln.

Davis, W. S. (1960). *A Day in Old Athens; a Picture of Athenian Life*. New York: Biblo & Tannen.

Department for Education (2014). *Statutory Framework for the Early Years Foundation Stage: Setting the Standards for Learning, Development and Care for Children from Birth to Five*. Available online: www.gov.uk/government/publications [Accessed: 14 July 2015].

Dewey, J. (1963). *Experience and Education*. New York: Collier Books.

Dewey, J. (2012). *Democracy and Education: An Introduction to the Philosophy of Education*. Los Angeles, CA: Indo-European Publishing.

Dodd, B. and Gillon, G. (2001). Exploring the relationship between phonological awareness, speech impairment and literacy. *Advances in Speech Language Pathology, 3(2)*, 139–147.

Droit-Volet, S., Fayolle S. L., and Gil, S. (2011). Emotion and time perception: effects of film-induced mood. *Frontiers in Integrative Neurosciences, 5*, 33.

Ebner, K. (2005). *Health and Healing through Water.* Available online: https://scholarsbank. uoregon.edu/xmlui/handle/1794/1916 [Accessed: 20 January 2014].

Ehri, L. (2004). Teaching phonemic awareness and phonics in P. McCardle. and L. Chhabra (eds), *The Voice of Evidence in Reading Research.* Baltimore, MD: Brookes Publishing Company.

Forman, George. (1999). Instant video revisiting: The video camera as a 'tool of the mind' for young children. *Early Childhood Research and Practice, 1(2).* Available online: http://ecrp. illinois.edu/v1n2/forman.html [Accessed: 5 July 2015].

Frost, J. (2006). *The Dissolution of Children's Outdoor Play: Causes and Consequences.* Available online: http://www.fairplayforchildren.org/pdf/1291334551.pdf [Accessed: 6 March 2009].

Frumkin, H. S. (2001). Beyond toxicity: Human health and the natural environment. *American Journal of Preventive Medicine, 20*, 234–240.

Gardner, H. (1985). *Frames of Mind: The Theory of Multiple Intelligences.* New York: Basic Books.

Genette, G. (1982). *Figures of Literary Discourse.* Available online: http://www19.homepage. villanova.edu/silvia.nagyzekmi/teoria2010/genette_frontiers_of_narrative.pdf [Accessed: 5 July 2015].

Gibbons, M. and Hopkins, D. (1980). How experiential is your experience-based program? *The Journal of Experiential Education, 3(1).*

Gibbons, M. and Hopkins, D. (1986). How experiential is your experience-based program? In R. Kraft and M. Sakofs (eds), *The Theory of Experiential Education* (pp. 135–140). Boulder, CO: Association for Experiential Education.

Gill, T. (2009). 'Now for free-range childhood', in *The Guardian*, 2 April 2009. Available online: www.guardian.co.uk/commentisfree/2009/apr/02/children-safety [Accessed: 21 September 2015].

Grandin, T. 2000. My mind is a web browser: How people with Autism think. *Cerebrum*, 2(1), 14–22.

Gronning, T., Singer, T, and Sohl, P. (2007). A.R.A.S. Archetypal Symbolism and Images. *Visual Resources, 23(3)*, 245–267.

Guillory, J. (1995). Literature, Culture, Politics. In F. Lentricchia and T. McLaughlin (eds), *Critical Terms for Literary Study.* Chicago, IL: The University of Chicago Press.

Hahn, K. (1957). Origins of the outward bound trust. In D. James (ed.), *Outward Bound* (pp. 1–17). London: Routledge and Kegan Paul.

Hattie, J. A. (1992). Measuring the effects of schooling. *Australian Journal of Education, 36*, 5–13.

Hattie, J. A., Marsh, H. W., Neill, J. T., and Richards, G. E. (1997). Adventure education and outward bound: Out-of-class experiences that have a lasting effect. *Review of Educational Research, 67*, 43–87.

Hendrick, J. (1996). *The Whole Child: Developmental Education for the Early Years.* Columbus, OH: Prentice-Hall.

Horton, R. and Hutchinson, S. (1997). *Nurturing Scientific Literacy among Youth through Experientially Based Curriculum Materials.* National Network for Science & Technology, USA. Available online: http://www.ohio4h.org/sites/ohio4h/files/d6/files/4H_591%20Nurturing %20Scientific%20Literacy%20Among%20Youth%20Through%20Experientially%20 Based%20Curriculum%20Materials.pdf [Accessed: 26 June 2015].

Horvath, J. (2010). Taking acceptable risks. *Early Years Educator, 12(7)*, 21–23.

Joplin, L. (1985). On defining experiential education. In R. Kraft and M. Sakofs (eds), *The Theory of Experiential Education.* Boulder, CO: Association for Experiential Education.

Jung, C. G. (1991). *The Archetypes and the Collective Unconscious* [sic], 2nd Edition, Collected Works of C. G. Jung. London: Routledge.

Kamii, C. and Russell, K. A. (2010). The older of two trees: Children's development of operational time. *Journal for Research in Mathematics Education*, 41(1), 6–13.

Keirsey. D. (1998). *Please Understand Me: 2*. Toronto: Prometheus Nemesis Book Co.

Kimball, R. O. and Bacon, S. B. (1993). The wilderness challenge model. In M. A. Gass (ed.), *Adventure Therapy: Therapeutic Applications of Adventure Programming* (pp. 11–41). Dubuque, IA: Kendall/Hunt.

King's Psychology Network (n.d.) Available online: http://www.psyking.net/id224.htm [Accessed: 27 June 2015].

Kloss, Jethro (1939). *Back to Eden*. Loma Linda, CA: Back to Eden Books.

Koestler A. (1964). *The Act of Creation*. New York: Penguin Books.

Kolb, D. A. (1984). *Experiential Learning: Experience as the Source of Learning and Development*. Englewood Cliffs, NJ: Prentice-Hall.

Lang, A. (2010). *The Pink Fairy Book*. Los Angeles, CA: Indo-European Publishing.

Learning + Teaching Scotland (2005). Available online: http://www.educationscotland.gov.uk/images/talkpedagogy_tcm4-193218.pdf [Accessed 15 July 2014].

Lees, C. and Hopkins, J. (2013). Effect of Aerobic Exercise on Cognition, Academic Achievement, and Psychosocial Function in Children: A Systematic Review of Randomized Control Trials. *Preventing Chronic Disease*, 10, E174.

Levi, D. M. and Klein, S.A. (2000). Seeing circles: What limits shape perception? *Vision Research*, 40(17), 2329–2339.

'Life's a Beach' Education Resource. Available online: http://www.boprc.govt.nz/residents/teachers/teacher-resources/lifes-a-beach-education-resource/ [Accessed: 5 July 2015].

Liset, G. (2006). *Sensory Motor Learning: Developing a Kinaesthetic Sense in the Throws*. Available online: http://www.coachr.org/sensory_motor_learning.htm [Accessed: 5 July 2015].

Little H. and Wyver, S. (2008). Outdoor play: Does avoiding the risks reduce the benefits? *Australian Journal of Early Childhood*, 33(2), 33–40.

Longenecker, R. N. (1982). The Pedagogical Nature of the Law in Galatians 3:19–4:7. *Journal of the Evangelical Theological Society*, 25.

Looman J. and Pillen H. (1989). The development of the bathing culture [in Dutch]. *Integraal*, 4, 7–24.

Lowry, C. A., Hollis, J. H., de Vries, A., Pan, B., Brunet, L. R., Hunt, J. R. F., van Kampen, E., Knight, D. M., Evans, A. K., Rook, G. A. W., and Lightman, S. L. (2007). Identification of an immune-responsive mesolimbocortical serotonergic system: potential role in regulation of emotional behavior. *Neuroscience*, 146 (2), 756–772.

Maller, C., Townsend, M., St Leger, L., Henderson-Wilson, C., Pryor, A., Prosser, L. and Moor, M. (2002). *Healthy Parks, Healthy People. The Health Benefits of Contact With Nature in a Park Context*. Melbourne: Deakin University and Parks Victoria. Available online: http://www.georgewright.org/262maller.pdf [Accessed 21 September 2015].

Martin, P. (1998). Education ideology and outdoor education. *Australian Journal of Outdoor Education*, 3(1), 14–20.

Meltzoff, A. (1988). Infant imitation after 1-week delay: Long-Term memory for novel acts and multiple stimuli. *Developmental Psychology*, 24(4), 470–476.

Menzies, H. (2005). *No Time: Stress and Crisis of Modern Life*. Vancouver, Canada: Douglas & McIntyre.

Miller, R. (n.d.). *A Brief Introduction to Holistic Education*. Available online: http://infed.org/mobi/a-brief-introduction-to-holistic-education/ [Accessed 27 June 2015].

Moss, S. (n.d.). *Create Your Own Wildlife Garden*. Available online: http://www.somersetwildlife.org/wildlife-gardening_old.html [Accessed 27 June 2015].

Myers, I.B. and McCaulley, M.H. (1985). *Manual: A Guide to the Development and Use of the Myers-Briggs Type Indicator*. Palo Alto, CA: Consulting Psychologists Press,

National Foundation for Educational Research (2007). Available online: http://www.nfer. ac.uk/research/projects/narrowing-the-gap/ [Accessed: 15 July 2015].

Neill, J. T. (2004). *A Psycho-Evolutionary Theory of Outdoor Education.* Available online: http://wilderdom.com/psycho-evolutionary/ [Accessed: 20 January 2014].

Neill, J. T. (2005). *Nature Theory.* Available online: http://www.wilderdom.com/theory/ NatureTheory.html [Accessed: 26 June 2015].

Neill, J. T. and Richards, G. E. (1998). Does outdoor education really work? A summary of recent meta-analysis. *Australian Journal of Outdoor Education,* 3(1).

Neill, J. T. and Dias, K. L. (2001). Adventure education and resilience – the double-edged sword. *Journal of Adventure Education and Outdoor Leadership,* 1(2), 35–42.

Nicholson, S. (1972). The theory of loose parts, an important principle for design methodology, *Studies in Design Education Craft and Technology,* 4(2).

O'Grady, P. (2000) *Internet Encyclopedia of Philosophy.* Available online: http://www.iep. utm.edu/thales/ [Accessed: 26 June 2015].

Phillpotts, E. (1919). *A Shadow Passes.* London: Macmillan.

Piaget, J. (1927/71). *The Child's Conception of Time.* New York: Ballantine Books.

Piaget, J. (1945). *Play, Dreams, and Imitation in Childhood.* New York: Norton.

Piaget, J. and Inhelder, B. (1969). *The Psychology of the Child.* New York: Basic Books.

Plato (1925). *Lysis* 208 C, trans. W. R. M. Lamb, Loeb Classical Library. Cambridge, MA: Harvard University Press.

Prayon Songsilp (1999). *Study and Analysis of Khmer Legends and Folk Tales, Regions 1–9.* Bangkok: Thai Language Field of Study, Faculty of Human and Social Sciences, Thonburi Rajabhat Institute. Available online: http://www.thaifolk.com/doc/literate/tales/reference_e. htm [Accessed: 20 January 2014].

Riechmann, S. W. and Grasha, A. F. (1974). A rational approach to developing and assessing the construct validity of a student learning styles instrument. *Journal of Psychology,* 87(2), 213–223.

Rinaldi, Carlina. (1998). Projected curriculum constructed through documentation – Progettazione: An interview with Lella Gandini in Carolyn Edwards, Lella Gandini, and George Forman (eds), *The Hundred Languages of Children: The Reggio Emilia Approach – Advanced Reflections,* 2nd edn (pp. 113–126). Greenwich, CT: Ablex.

Rivkin, M. (1995). *The Great Outdoors: Restoring Children's Rights to Play Outside.* Washington, DC: NAEYC.

Robinson, K. and Aronica, L. (2009). *The Element.* London: Penguin.

Rudd M., Vohs K. D., and Aaker J. (2012). Awe expands people's perception of time, alters decision making, and enhances well-being. *Psychological Science,* 23(10): 1130–1136.

Sandseter, E. B. H. (2007). Categorising risky play – how can we identify risk-taking in children's play? *European Early Childhood Education Research Journal,* 15(2), 237–252.

Sargent, M. (2011). *The Project Approach in the Early Years Provision: A Practical Guide to Developing a Child-Centred Curriculum.* London: Practical Preschool Books.

Scherl, L. M. (1988). Constructions of a wilderness experience: Using the repertory grid technique in the natural setting. *Australian Psychologist,* 23(2), 225–242.

Smith. M. K. (2012). *What is Pedagogy?* Available online: http://infed.org/mobi/what-is-pedagogy/ [Accessed 3 May 2014].

Smith, T. (2005). *Play and Playthings: How It Affects the Learning Process.* East Lansing, MI: Michigan State University.

Steiner, R. (1965). *The Education of the Child in the Light of Anthroposophy.* London: Rudolf Steiner Press.

Stevens, A. (2003). *Archetype Revisited: an Updated Natural History of the Self.* Toronto, ON: Inner City Books.

Tilbury, D. and Wortman, D. (2004). *Engaging People in Sustainability.* Gland, Switzerland: IUCN.

Tovey, H. (2008), *Playing Outdoors: Spaces and Places, Risk and Challenges*. Berkshire: Open University Press.

UK Biodiversity Action Plan 1994. Available online: http://jncc.defra.gov.uk/PDF/UKBAP_Action-Plan-1994.pdf [Accessed: 1 July 2015].

UK Essays (2013). *Outdoor Play in Early Years*. Available online: http://www.ukessays.com/essays/young-people/investigation-of-outdoor-play-in-early-years-young-people-essay.php [Accessed 3 February 2014].

Verstegen, I. (2005). *Arnheim, Gestalt and Art: A Psychological Theory*. New York: Springer.

Warden, C. (2007). *Nurture through Nature*. Perthshire, Scotland: Mindstretchers.

Wildlife Trusts. Available online: http://www.wildlifetrusts.org/wildlife/habitat-explorer [Accessed 27 June 2015].

Wilson, E. O. (1984). *Biophilia: The Human Bond with Other Species*. Cambridge, MA: Harvard University Press.

Index

mud 40; natural forces 42; natural
learning 53–55; New Zealand 115;
physical well-being 70–71; risk taking
98; schemas 81–82; session overview
61–64; special educational needs 82–89;
student-led 10; teaching methodology
49–50; understanding concepts 77–78;
water-sensing procedure 60–61; *see also*
pedagogy
learning styles 28–29, 30, 43–49, 56
Levi, D. M. 87
'Life's a Beach' 114–115
light 38, 42–43, 76
limits, setting 34, 86
links 51, 52
listener, adult as 32
literacy 59, 65, 66
littoral zone 17–18, 19
Locke, John 76
'loose parts' theory 35–36
lost child procedures 94
low tide zone 20
lowland rivers 14–15
Lowry, Chris 40

The Magic Spring (folk tale) 6
magnifying glasses 75
Malaguzzi, Loris 105
Malting House School 26
mapping 78
marks 73–75
Marsh, H. W. 10
marshes 18
Martin, Peter 8
masks 75, 86–87
mathematics 7, 40, 59, 66, 78
McMillan, Margaret 26
'me by me' observation method 56
measuring 7, 40, 78
memories 50–51, 53, 60, 63, 82
mentor, adult as 31–32
Menzies, H. 39
message in a bottle 74
metaphors 29, 73–74
middle tide zone 20
milestone observations 80–81
Miller, Ron 59
mirror, water as a 68
mistakes 40
mobiles 68–69
model making 71

Montessori, Maria 26
moral development 65
moss 21
Moss, S. 20
motivation 23, 53, 60, 72, 89
MOTIVE approach 79
motor skills 70, 71
MOTORS 79–80
movement observation tool 58
mud 40, 59, 67–68, 71, 76, 77, 83
mudflats 20
music 76, 77, 83, 86
Myers-Briggs Type Indicator 44

narrator, adult as 31
natural forces 41–42, 111
natural learning 53–55
natural materials 28, 30, 40–43, 59, 72;
Froebel approach 113; 'loose parts' 35–36;
play therapy 86; *see also* pebbles; sand;
sticks
nature: Denmark 113; freedom and order
26, 27; Froebel approach 113; natural
forces 41–42, 111; Process of Nature
Encounter 36–37, 45; Reggio Emilia
approach 106; Shelter-Plant-Animal 88;
Steiner on 108; Thales' philosophy 25;
types of experience with 34–35; Waldorf
Családi Napközi 108
nature-colour-copying 76
nature education theories 7–10, 23
Nature Kindergartens, Scotland 111–112
Nature Relations Style 45
nature table 108
neap tides 96–97
Neill, James 7, 8, 9–10
networking 104
New Zealand 114–115
Nicholson, Simon 35
note taker, adult as 33

objects 68–69, 74, 113
observation: adult as observer 32; Denmark
114; field-based observation tool 55–56;
'me by me' observation method 56;
milestones 80–81; movement observation
tool 58; New Zealand 115; numerical
scale of Water School behaviour 57–58;
observational learning 46, 54, 55; water-
pebble storycrafting 87; Water School
interaction method 56–57